DRESDEN
CARNIVAL

16 MODERN QUILT PROJECTS
-•- INNOVATIVE DESIGNS -•-

MARIAN B. GALLIAN *and*
YVETTE MARIE JONES

stashBOOKS.
an imprint of C&T Publishing

Text copyright © 2016 by Marian Barbara Gallian and Yvette Marie Jones

Photography and artwork copyright © 2016 by C&T Publishing, Inc.

PUBLISHER:
Amy Marson

CREATIVE DIRECTOR:
Gailen Runge

EDITOR:
Lynn Koolish

TECHNICAL EDITORS:
Debbie Rodgers and
Deanna Csomo McCool

COVER/BOOK DESIGNER:
April Mostek

PRODUCTION COORDINATOR / ILLUSTRATOR:
Freesia Pearson Blizard

PRODUCTION EDITORS:
Joanna Burgarino, Jessie Brotman, and
Jennifer Warren

PHOTO ASSISTANT:
Sarah Frost

STYLE PHOTOGRAPHY by Page + Pixel and
INSTRUCTIONAL PHOTOGRAPHY by Diane Pedersen,
unless otherwise noted

Published by Stash Books, an imprint of C&T Publishing, Inc., P.O. Box 1456,
Lafayette, CA 94549

Library of Congress Cataloging-in-Publication Data

Names: Gallian, Marian B., 1946- author. | Jones, Yvette Marie, 1978- author.

Title: Dresden carnival : 16 modern quilt projects - innovative designs / Marian B.
Gallian and Yvette Marie Jones.

Description: Lafayette, CA : C&T Publishing, 2016.

Identifiers: LCCN 2015039022 | ISBN 9781617450853 (soft cover)

Subjects: LCSH: Patchwork--Patterns. | Appliquâe--Patterns. | Quilting--Patterns. |
Dresden plate quilts.

Classification: LCC TT835 .G3315 2016 | DDC 746.46--dc23

LC record available at http://lccn.loc.gov/2015039022

Printed in China

10 9 8 7 6 5 4 3 2 1

DEDICATION

This book is dedicated to Grams, Marian's mother and Yvette's grandmother, Esther Marian Olson Howard (1915–2004). Esther was born in northern Minnesota in a small Norwegian fishing village and later moved to a farm. It was there that she learned about hard work and the arts of cooking and sewing. She moved to Washington, D.C. in 1936 and worked for the Department of the Navy. There she met and married her husband, Army Captain Richmond Howard. Grams was very active in both her daughter's and her seven grandchildren's lives. She is most remembered for her love of gardening, her sewing, and her baking skills—especially her chocolate cake.

ACKNOWLEDGMENTS

The love, support, and encouragement we have received from our family and friends has been invaluable.

Our heartfelt thanks:

To Matthew, who believed in what we could accomplish and encouraged us to achieve our dreams.

To Pierce and Ella, for their sweet encouragement, support, and unwavering faith in us.

To Cherie and Lisa, who have been our constant cheerleaders every step along the way.

To Joey, Rusty, Jason, Ryan, and all my grandchildren who enjoy their quilted treasures and support our efforts.

To Nancy Butler and Kathryn Carbine, for sharing their skills and talents to help make the beautiful quilts in this book.

To Riley Blake Designs, Makower UK, and Michael Miller Fabrics for providing us with beautiful fabrics to make the quilts in this book.

To C&T Publishing, for their encouragement and support of new authors. They have made every step of this process enjoyable.

Contents

Dresden Carnival

Introduction

Summer is our favorite season because it is filled with so much warmth, memories, and joy—just like our treasured heirloom quilts. We have taken inspiration from some of our favorite summer memories, such as visiting the fair to ride on a Ferris wheel and eat cotton candy, or sipping cool lemonade during a heat wave. We turned those memories into quilt designs featuring variations of the Dresden Plate.

Our book explores all dimensions of the historic Dresden Plate block—from innovative, modern designs to playful color choices and exciting new borders. This book has a quilt that is perfect for everyone and is sure to bring back memories of your favorite summers spent with those you love.

We are also passionate about appliqué and have used it extensively in the designs of these quilts. Appliqué is not just a skill for your current project, but it is a journey that will last for a lifetime. It is a time-honored art form, and we are sure if you look into your family history, you will find a lady that did fine stitching in your past. And maybe she even did it while sitting peacefully in the shade of her garden on a warm summer day surrounded by daisies.

APPLIQUÉ BASICS

Needle-turn appliqué is one of the original and most traditional methods of appliqué. We prefer this method because it is very portable and requires very little preparation. The finished edges and extra dimension you get from turning under the edges also give the quilt a polished finish.

Tools and Supplies

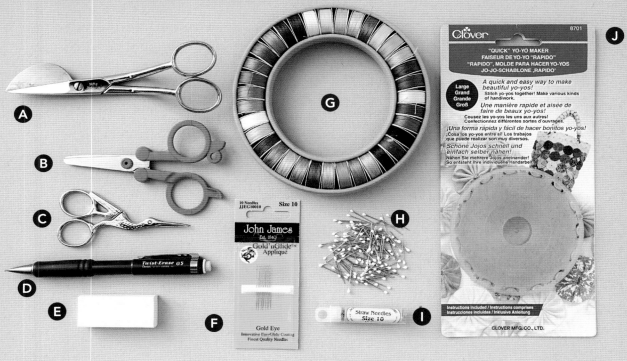

A. Appliqué scissors

B. Airplane-compatible scissors

C. Small embroidery scissors

D. Mechanical pencil

E. Extra Soft White Vinyl Eraser from General Pencil Company

F. John James Gold'nGlide appliqué needles

G. Superior Threads MasterPiece cotton thread

H. Short appliqué pins

I. Straw needles from Jeana Kimball's Foxglove Cottage

J. Clover Quick Yo-Yo Maker

NEEDLES

Many opinions vary on hand appliqué needles, but we like the John James Gold'nGlide appliqué needles made in England. The threading is easier because the eye of the needle is larger. The company has combined the excellent quality of English needles with their Gold'nGlide coating. They have applied 18–karat gold to the needle to gild the eyes for easier threading, fast stitching, and less stress on your hands as the needle glides through the fabric.

We also like the straw needles from Jeana Kimball's Foxglove Cottage. These needles have a narrow shank that allows them to glide through the fabric. The eye of the needle is punched through the existing shank of the needle, so the needle doesn't hesitate at the eye when going through fabric.

Other good needle choices are sharps, which are long, thin needles that are perfect for appliqué work. Straw and milliners needles are popular choices also. It is important to choose a needle size that's comfortable in your hand.

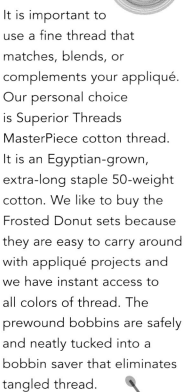

THREAD

It is important to use a fine thread that matches, blends, or complements your appliqué. Our personal choice is Superior Threads MasterPiece cotton thread. It is an Egyptian-grown, extra-long staple 50-weight cotton. We like to buy the Frosted Donut sets because they are easy to carry around with appliqué projects and we have instant access to all colors of thread. The prewound bobbins are safely and neatly tucked into a bobbin saver that eliminates tangled thread.

PINS

We always use short appliqué pins for securing appliqués to the background before stitching. They hold the appliqué more securely and don't interfere with your thread as much as longer pins. You are also less likely to get poked when using these pins.

SCISSORS

Small embroidery scissors are a good investment. They have razor-sharp edges and pointed tips that are great for clipping into deep valleys and rounded curves. They are also perfect for making precise trims and cutting into areas that might need to be coaxed to turn under.

Appliqué scissors traditionally have a paddle blade on one side that resembles a duck bill. When you trim edges, the paddle pushes the seam allowance out of the way to keep you from cutting too close.

Airplane-compatible scissors deserve a mention. Doing appliqué while waiting in an airport or while flying will bring you peace on a stressful travel day. Always look up the current Transportation Security Administration (TSA) rules, but generally a small, folding scissor with a very short blade and a blunt tip can be used (less than 4″ in length).

MARKING TOOLS

We like to use mechanical pencils when marking quilts because they have been used for ages and have never ruined a quilt. Also, you never have to sharpen them. The marks can be erased with a good, soft eraser. Lots of fabric erasers are on the market, and I recommend the Extra Soft White Vinyl Eraser from General Pencil Company (available at most art supply stores). Erasers on the tip of pencils rarely remove pencil from fabric.

Alternatively, you can use removable markers, but keep in mind that some of these marks disappear with heat, moisture, or time, and if you don't finish your quilt right away, your markings may disappear. Also, some marks become permanent when ironed, so take care when using removable markers. Disappearing-ink pens require that you wash your blocks or quilt to remove the chemicals from the fabric. Just getting it wet will remove the marks, but not the chemicals.

TEMPLATE MATERIALS

You can make sturdy templates of the appliqué shapes using template plastic, several sheets of freezer paper ironed together, cardboard from a cereal box, or clear plastic adhesive laminate placed on top of a copy of the appliqué pattern.

Appliqué Techniques

MAKING TEMPLATES

Create a template for each appliqué shape in your selected project using the patterns provided in the book. Regardless of how you make the templates, compare them with the originals in the book to make sure they are accurate.

- For see-through plastic, place the plastic over the patterns and trace the images. Cut out the templates.

- For plastic laminate, make a copy of the needed patterns from the book, and place the laminate on top of the patterns. Cut out the templates.

- For other template materials, make a copy of the patterns from the book, cut them out, and trace around them on the template material. Cut out the templates.

USING TEMPLATES

Place the templates on the selected fabrics and draw around them. If possible, draw all the shapes side-by-side and cut them out on the outer drawn line.

Note: The patterns in this book include a 1/4˝ seam or turn-under allowance.

TIP Make it easier to draw around templates on fabric by placing your fabric on a sandboard first. The sandboard will hold on to the fabric so it doesn't move while you draw (refer to Resources, page 103).

SEWING DRESDEN PETALS TOGETHER

The petals are sewn together before they are appliquéd. Each petal has straight sides, a curved or pointed top, and a narrow end.

1. Place 2 petals right sides together. Start at the top of a straight side and sew 3 stitches, backstitch to the top, and then sew straight to the bottom of the 2 petals.

This way you will have no dangling threads or weakness when you clip the threads at the top of the petals. Accuracy is very important here, as you will be appli- quéing the curved edges.

2. Add additional petals in the same way.

3. Press the seams in one direction and block using the provided pressing guide (refer to Pressing and Blocking, page 12).

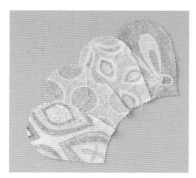

MAKING DRESDEN BLOCKS

1. For larger appliqués, fold the background in half from top to bottom and finger-press. Unfold and fold again from side to side. Finger-press. Unfold. Fold along each diagonal, making finger creases each time. These fold lines will help you arrange the appliqués on the background fabric.

2. For intricate blocks, trace the provided layout on top of the fabric to use as a placement guide—use a fine lead pencil, placing lines slightly inward from the target spot for fabric motifs, or trace with one of the many disappearing-ink pens on the market. *Note:* Read the instructions that come with the pen so you know how to remove the marks.

3. Pin or baste motifs to the block, starting with the bottom layer. You don't need to appliqué edges that are covered by other shapes (but we like to tack them down). You can pin all of the shapes to the block now, or work in layers from the back forward (our favorite).

4. Appliqué the motifs in place.

NEEDLE TURN APPLIQUÉ

Use a blind stitch for appliqué.

1. Begin by tucking the fabric under at the drawn line with your needle and holding it in place with your thumbnail.

2. Using your other hand, bring the needle up from the bottom through 1–3 threads on the edge of the appliqué.

3. Bring the needle down into the background fabric right where you initially came up. Do not pass through the appliqué again. Use the tip or the side of the needle to fold under the seam allowance just beyond this stitch, taking care to hide the mark under the fold.

4. Repeat, bringing the needle up from the bottom ⅛˝ away and through the appliqué again.

5. Tug the thread slightly to make your stitches disappear into the background and edge of the motif.

6. Continue folding and sewing all around the appliqué.

7. When you reach the end, take the needle through the background and make a small stitch, leaving a loop. Thread the needle through the loop and pull to create a knot. Bury the tail of the thread between the layers of the background and the appliqué.

Optional: Some quilters cut away the excess fabric under the appliqué, leaving only the top layer and a ½˝ (or so) rim of fabric around the shapes on the reverse side of the block. This eliminates bulk. Other quilters feel that leaving it in gives stability to the motif.

HELPFUL STITCHING TIPS

- Thread your needle with about 18˝–20˝ of cotton thread, usually about the length from your fingertips to your elbow.

- Cut your thread with sharp scissors at a 45° angle.

- Always thread your needle with the end you've just cut.

- Always tie a knot in the end you just cut.

- As you hand sew, pull the thread in the direction you are sewing to reduce tangling.

- Use one strand of thread when appliquéing.

- Some quilters like to twist the needle between their fingers to unwind the thread as they stitch in the opposite direction of the twist of the thread.

- You can use dryer sheets to help prevent static cling and tangling. Just run your thread between the layers of a folded dryer sheet a couple of times.

- It is best to go a shade lighter if you are appliquéing to a light background, or a shade darker if you are appliquéing to a dark background.

STITCHING CONCAVE CURVES

Concave curves are like a smiling face. When appliquéing, it is easier to turn under the edge if you clip along the curve. Stop clipping about 2–3 threads from the seamline.

STITCHING CONVEX CURVES

Convex curves are like a frowning face. There is no need to make any adjustments because the fabric will naturally curve. Taking smaller stitches will make a smoother curve.

Concave curves

STITCHING OUTWARD POINTS

If you look at a triangle, the corners are all outward points. These points can become bulky when all of the fabric around the point is turned under to fit in a very small space.

1. Stitch up to the point and take 1 extra stitch in place right at the point where the next seam line intersects. Cut off the dog ear.

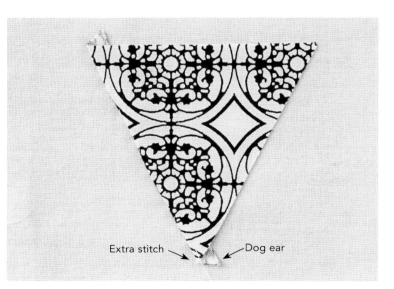

Extra stitch   Dog ear

2. Grade the seam beneath your stitching and trim or blunt the point.

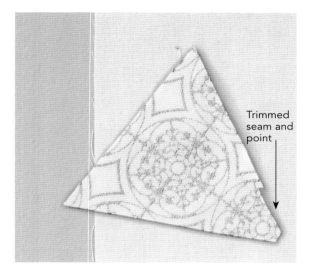

Trimmed seam and point

3. Fold the point straight back.

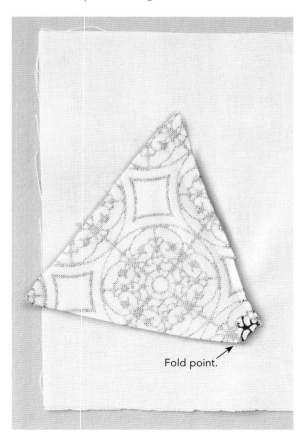

Fold point.

4. Turn the point 45° and take 1 stitch in place, giving it a slight tug to maintain the sharp point.

5. Finish sweeping the fabric neatly under and take 1 more stitch in place, giving it another slight tug, and continue stitching up the side.

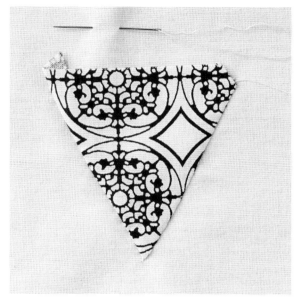

STITCHING INSIDE POINTS

Before you get to an inside point, use small scissors to clip close to the seamline. Use your needle to turn under the seam allowance. Take a little deeper stitch at the very inside point or several stitches very close together. Evaluate your design and, if necessary, alter the design so the point is not so deep.

REVERSE APPLIQUÉ

With reverse appliqué, the top layer of fabric is cut away to reveal the fabric underneath. Both fabrics should be right side up.

1. Draw the appliqué on the top fabric with a pencil. Mark the cutting line inside the appliqué line about ¼".

2. Cut out on the ¼" line without cutting through the bottom layer of fabric. If the appliqué has inside curves, clip them to within 3 strands of the appliqué line.

3. Sweep the fabric under the stitching line as in regular appliqué and stitch it in place.

SHADOWING

When you appliqué a light fabric over a dark fabric, oftentimes the dark fabric will show through. After you are done appliquéing, trim the darker fabric away ¼" inside the stitching line.

PRESSING AND BLOCKING

Blocking is done by pressing sewn-together petals using a pressing guide; it sets the stitches and standardizes the final shape and size.

To create a pressing guide, print out the pressing guide for the project and place a scrap piece of fabric over it on a lightbox or bright window. Trace the pattern onto the fabric with a permanent marker. Place the fabric pressing guide on your ironing board, pin each group of petals in place, and iron them into shape.

It is important to maintain the overall spacing in your design so that the Dresden center will fit the opening. Because of the bias edges in these Dresden blocks, distortion from normal sewing and pressing is not uncommon.

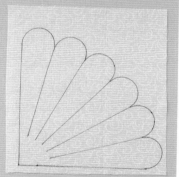

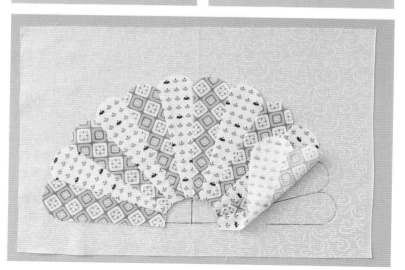

YO-YOS

Yo-yos are a great way to add texture and dimension to a project.

Use matching buttonhole or quilting thread (preferred) or a double strand of sewing thread (we have used black thread for the pictures). Make sure you have a large knot at the end of the thread and enough thread to go all the way around the edge of the circle.

1. Cut out a circle of fabric that is 2 times larger plus ¼˝ than the finished yo-yo.

2. Finger-press under ¼˝ and make a running stitch around the edge, starting on the inside and ending on the outside beside the first stitch. The bigger the spaces between your stitches, the tighter the circle becomes when you are finished.

3. Pull the string and work the fabric into a neat, evenly pleated circle.

4. Pull the thread across the circle to get the tightest knot.

5. Run the thread through half of the folds one more time, maintaining tension.

6. Pull the thread through the center of the bottom and knot securely before cutting the thread.

TIP Our favorite way to make yo-yos is to use the Clover Quick Yo-Yo Maker.

PERFECT CIRCLES

You will need fabric, a piece of aluminum foil, a template that will tolerate high heat, and a pencil.

1. Trace a circle on the back side of the selected fabric.

2. Cut out the fabric with a scant ¼˝ seam allowance.

3. Cut a piece of foil a little larger than the cut-out fabric.

4. Put the shiny side of the foil facedown, place the fabric facedown on top of the foil, and center the template on the fabric.

5. Put your thumb in the middle and fold the foil around the circle template, nice and tight.

6. Turn it over and make sure you don't have any creases on the edge.

7. With the smooth side facing up on the ironing board, press for 5 seconds with the iron.

8. Give it a few minutes to cool and open it up for a perfect circle ready to appliqué.

CENTIPEDE

Inspired by fuzzy caterpillars inching along thin branches, we alternated half-Dresdens up and down to imitate the undulating pattern of a crawling caterpillar. Fabric selection is the key ingredient in this quilt as it was designed to be used with a line of coordinating fabrics that comes in three colorways. All three of the colorways are blended in the quilt: one with a gold background, one with peach, and one with green. The intermingling of the dot fabrics ties them together.

MATERIALS

Dots in 3 different colorways: ⅝ yard each

Large print in 3 different colorways: ¼ yard each

Small print in 3 different colorways: ¼ yard each

Geometric print in 3 different colorways: ¼ yard each

Stripe: 1 yard for border 1 and binding

White: 4 yards for background and border 2

Backing: 4⅓ yards

Batting: 77″ × 82″

Skill level:
beginner

Finished quilt:
69" × 74"

Finished block:
9" × 9"

CUTTING

Appliqué

Make templates A, B, and C using the *Centipede* patterns (pullout pages P2 and P4). Refer to Making Templates (page 7) as needed.

- Cut 15 using semicircle B, 5 from each of the 3 dot colorways.

- Cut 6 using quarter-circle C, 2 from each of the 3 dot colorways.

- Cut 144 using petal A, 12 from each of the 3 colorways of dots, large prints, small prints, and geometrics.

Background

- Cut 36 white squares 9½″ × 9½″.

- Cut 3 white sashing strips 1½″ × width of fabric, sew end to end, and cut 2 rectangles 1½″ × 54½″.

- Cut 2 sashing strips 1½″ × width of fabric from each colorway of dots, sew each pair together end to end, and cut 2 rectangles 1½″ × 54½″.

Border 1

- Cut 6 border 1 stripe strips 1½″ × width of fabric, sew end to end, and cut 2 borders 1½″ × 54½″ and 2 borders 1½″ × 61½″.

Border 2

- Cut 7 border 2 white strips 6¾″ × width of fabric, sew end to end, and cut 2 borders 6¾″ × 56½″ and 2 borders 6¾″ × 74″.

Construction

SEW TOGETHER THE PETALS

1. Sew the petals together in the order and quantity as indicated (refer to Sewing Dresden Petals Together, page 8).

2. After the petals are sewn together, press them using the *Centipede* pressing guide (pullout page P4). Refer to Pressing and Blocking (page 12).

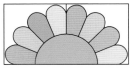

Make 1.   Make 1.   Make 5.

Make 1.   Make 1.   Make 5.

Make 1.   Make 1.   Make 5.

Designed and made by Marian Gallian, quilted by Kathryn Carbine
Fabric: Cottage Garden by Lila Tueller for Riley Blake Designs

Centipede **17**

ASSEMBLE THE BLOCKS

1. Appliqué the petal sets to the background squares (refer to Needle Turn Appliqué, page 8).

2. For each colorway, sew 5 pairs of blocks together.

3. Appliqué the semicircles and quarter-circles to the petal sets.

4. Sew the blocks together into rows. Then sew the rows and sashing strips together as in the quilt assembly diagram on the next page.

MAKE THE BORDERS

Press after adding each border.

Border 1

1. Sew the 1½″ × 54½″ borders to the top and bottom of the quilt.

2. Sew the 1½″ × 61½″ borders to the right and left of the quilt.

Border 2

1. Sew 2 borders 6¾″ × 56½″ to the top and bottom of the quilt.

2. Sew the 2 borders 6¾″ × 74″ to the right and left of the quilt.

FINISHING THE QUILT

1. Layer the quilt top, batting, and backing.

2. Quilt as desired.

3. Bind using your favorite method or refer to Bonus Technique: Binding (page 100).

4. Make a label and sew it on the back of the quilt.

Quilt assembly

PEEK-A-BOO VIOLETS

The modern simplicity of this quilt celebrates the simple pleasures of summer with flowers peeking out from behind the leaves.

MATERIALS

Light gray: ⅛ yard

Medium gray: ¼ yard

Light purple: ¾ yard

Medium purple: ¾ yard

Dark purple: 1½ yards

White 1: ¾ yard

White 2: ¾ yard

White 3: 3¼ yards for background

Backing: 4⅓ yards

Binding: ¾ yard

Batting: 76″ × 83″

CUTTING

Appliqué

Make templates A, B, C, and D using the *Peek-a-Boo Violets* patterns (pullout page P2). Refer to Making Templates (page 7) as needed.

- Cut 10 semicircles D from light gray.
- Cut 5 circles C from medium gray.
- Cut 30 petals A from medium purple.
- Cut 30 petals B from light purple.
- Cut 30 petals A from white 1.
- Cut 30 petals B from white 2.

Background

- Cut 1 white 3 piece 8″ × 75½″.
- Cut 1 white 3 piece 30½″ × 75½″.
- Cut 10 white 3 strips 8″ × 15½″.
- Cut 5 dark purple squares 15½″ × 15½″.

Peek-a-Boo Violets

Made by Marian Gallian and Nancy Butler, quilted by Kathryn Carbine

Construction

SEW TOGETHER THE PETALS

1. Sew the light purple and medium purple petals into semicircles of 6, alternating the colors to make 10 identical sets.

2. Press using the *Peek-a-Boo Violets* pressing guide (pullout page P2). Refer to Pressing and Blocking (page 12).

3. Center and appliqué the purple semicircles to the white 8″ × 15½″ strips.

4. Appliqué the light gray semicircles to the petal sets.

5. Sew the white 1 and white 2 petals into circles of 12, alternating the shapes.

6. Center and appliqué the white circles to the purple 15½″ × 15½″ background squares to make 5 identical squares (refer to Stitching Concave Curves and Stitching Convex Curves, page 10).

7. Appliqué the dark gray circles to the petal sets.

ASSEMBLE THE QUILT

1. Sew the 8″ × 15½″ appliquéd background pieces together end to end into 2 strips, 5 in each of the strips. Press.

2. Sew the 5 purple appliquéd background squares together in a row. Press.

3. Sew the white strips on either side of the purple strip. Press.

4. Sew the 2 large background pieces to each side of the quilt. Press.

FINISH THE QUILT

1. Layer the quilt top, batting, and backing.

2. Quilt as desired.

3. Bind using your favorite method or refer to Bonus Technique: Binding (page 100).

4. Make a label and sew it on the back of the quilt.

Designed by Marian Gallian, made by Marian Gallian and Nancy Butler, quilted by Kathryn Carbine

COTTON CANDY PILLOW

A visit to the fair isn't complete without some cotton candy. Picture the cotton candy as it swirls around the cone in subtle gradations from dark to light. This combination of colors and swirling shapes makes a dynamic pillow.

MATERIALS

Medium pink: 3 pieces
⅛ yard or fat eighths

Medium-dark red: 3 pieces
⅛ yard or fat eighths

Medium-light pink: 3 pieces
⅛ yard or fat eighths

Light pink: 3 pieces
⅛ yard or fat eighths

Center circle: Scrap at least 5″ × 5″

Pillow top and back: ⅝ yard

Quilt backing: 1⅝ yards

Batting: 2 squares 28″ × 28″

Pillow form: 20″ × 20″

CUTTING

Appliqué

Make templates A, B, C, D, and E using the Cotton Candy Pillow patterns (pullout pages P1–P4). Refer to Making Templates (page 7) as needed.

- Cut 12 using petal A, 4 from each medium pink.
- Cut 12 using petal B, 4 from each red.
- Cut 12 using petal C, 4 from each medium-light pink.
- Cut 12 using petal D, 4 from each light pink.
- Cut 1 center circle E from scrap.

Pillow top and back

- Cut 2 squares 21″ × 21″.

Quilt backing

- Cut 2 squares 28″ × 28″.

Skill level:
confident
beginner

*Finished
pillow:*
20" × 20"

Construction

PREPARE THE PETALS

Refer to Needle Turn Appliqué (page 8) as needed.

Separate the petals into 3 groups of 1 medium pink, 1 medium-dark red, 1 medium-light pink, and 1 light pink. For each group make 4 complete petals as instructed below.

1. Appliqué petal part B on petal A. Cut away excess fabric underneath.

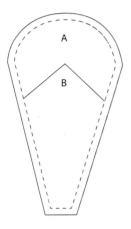

2. Appliqué petal part C on petal A/B. Cut away excess fabric underneath.

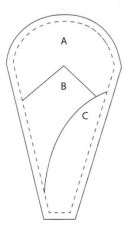

3. Appliqué petal part D on petal A/B/C. Cut away excess fabric underneath.

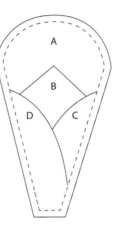

4. Sew the Dresden petals to form a circle (refer to Sewing Dresden Petals Together, page 8). Press.

5. Center the petal circle on the pillow top and appliqué (refer to Making Dresden Blocks, page 8, for centering technique).

6. Appliqué the center circle.

QUILTING THE PILLOW

1. Layer the pillow top and back, each with their own batting and backing for quilting. Quilt each piece as desired.

2. Trim quilted pillow pieces to 21″ × 21″.

PILLOW ASSEMBLY

1. On the pillow top and back, mark a dot ½″ inside each corner. Mark the center of each outside edge. Draw a straight line from the ½″ dot to the center.

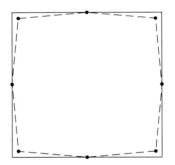

2. Cut along the drawn line. This small adjustment keeps the corners of the pillow from feeling unfilled.

Designed and made by Marian Gallian, quilted by Kathryn Carbine
Fabric: Make it scrappy using shades of light and dark pink and red on a white tone-on-tone background.

ALTERNATE COLORWAY: *Scandinavian Christmas Pillow*

Designed and made by Marian Gallian, quilted by Kathryn Carbine • *Fabric: Scandi Christmas by Makower UK*

3. Fold under the bottom edge of the pillow top ½˝ to the inside. Press and baste. Repeat for the pillow back. You will use the creases of these folds to guide you as you sew the pillow closed.

4. Place the pillow top and pillow back right sides together. Sew 3 sides with a ½˝ seam allowance, leaving the basted side open. Clip the corners and trim where needed. Turn right side out. Make sure the 2 corners are fully turned.

5. Insert the pillow form, making sure the pillow reaches into both inside corners.

6. Pin front and back together and hand stitch with matching thread using a ladder stitch (page 60) or a very small, tight whipstitch.

GARDEN PARTY

This quilt was inspired by children playing at a garden party, taking turns peering through a kaleidoscope at a beautifully blooming bush full of flowers. The fractured repetition of this technique makes for stunning and unique Dresdens.

MATERIALS

Fabric A: 4 pieces ⅓ yard each with same value for center background

Fabric B: 11 pattern repeats of focus fabric for petals, yo-yo centers, and borders 1 and 3

Fabric C: ⅝ yard for sashing and borders 2 and 5

Fabric D: ½ yard stripe for sashing and borders 2 and 5

Fabric E: 1⅞ yards for borders 4 and 6 and binding

Batting: 70″ × 70″

Backing: 4 yards

Note

All fabric is made by repeating the same pattern down the length of the fabric. Repeats can range anywhere from 4″ to 36″. Look for one in the center of that range—somewhere between 18″ and 24″. The larger the repeat of a floral or graphic design, the more diversity in your flower petals.

When selecting your focus fabric, note that stripes are harder to work with, as are fabrics with grids or boxes. The design for this quilt alternates 2 petals in each of the Dresden plate flowers. By cutting 2 sets of coordinating petals for each flower, you create a distinct design for each Dresden plate. Be sure there is sufficient contrast between the petals in each plate.

CUTTING

Make templates A and B using the *Garden Party* patterns (pullout page P3). Refer to Making Templates (page 7) as needed.

Dresden petals

1 Cut your focus fabric (fabric B) in half lengthwise and set aside one section.

2 Cut the width of the remaining fabric into 10 pattern repeats.

3 Stick the point of a pin through each layer at exactly the same location. Hold the pin from the bottom so that all the layers are perfected aligned and pin the layers together. Flower pins work best for this because they lie flat. Do this in a number of places throughout the fabric.

We suggest that you make 8 clear plastic petal templates so you can audition the shape in various places on the fabric that look interesting. Because you have a limited amount of fabric, all 8 templates should be placed on the fabric before cutting.

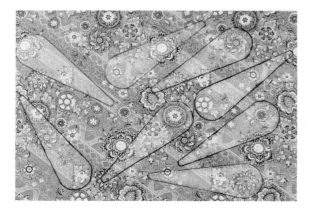

You now have a landscape from which to start. Because 10 layers will be difficult to cut through successfully, we recommend 2 identical sets of 5 layers. When the first petal set of 5 is cut, place each petal on the second fabric layer set and find the identical pattern to cut. When done you should have 10 each of 8 different petals.

Background

● Cut 4 squares 10½˝ × 10½˝ from each of the 4 fabric A pieces.

Yo-yo centers

● Cut 4 distinct yo-yo B circles from fabric B.

Border 1

From the remaining length of focus fabric:

● Cut 8 strips 1˝ × 20½˝.

● Cut 8 strips 1˝ × 21½˝.

Borders 2 and 5 (sashing)

● Cut 26 fabric C strips ¾˝ × width of fabric.

● Cut 13 fabric D strips 1˝ × width of fabric.

Center sashing intersection

● Cut 2 fabric C rectangles ¾˝ × 1½˝.

● Cut 2 fabric C squares ¾˝ × ¾˝.

● Cut 1 fabric D square 1˝ × 1˝.

Designed by Marian Gallian, made by Marian Gallian and Nancy Butler, quilted by Kathryn Carbine • *Fabric: Belle by Amy Butler was used for the focus and border prints.*

ALTERNATE COLORWAY: *Beach Party Quilt*

Designed by Marian Gallian, made by Nancy Butler, quilted by Kathryn Carbine
Fabric: Lark by Amy Butler

Sashing corners

- Cut 8 fabric C rectangles ¾″ × 1½″.
- Cut 8 fabric C rectangles ¾″ × 1¼″.
- Cut 8 fabric C squares ¾″ × ¾″.
- Cut 8 fabric D rectangles 1″ × 1¼″ (with stripe parallel to 1″ side).
- Cut 8 fabric D rectangles ¾″ × 1″ (with stripe parallel to 1″ side).

Border 3

- Cut 2 fabric B strips 1″ × 45½″ lengthwise.
- Cut 2 fabric B strips 1″ × 46½″ lengthwise.

Border 4

- Cut 5 fabric E strips 5¼″ × width of fabric, sew the strips end to end, and cut 2 borders 5¼″ × 46½″ and 2 borders 5¼″ × 56″.

Border 6

- Cut 6 fabric E strips 2½″ × width of fabric, sew the strips end to end, and cut 2 borders 2½″ × 58″ and 2 borders 2½″ × 62″.

Construction

ASSEMBLE THE BLOCK

1. Make 4 squares 20½″ × 20½″ from the 16 fabric A 10½″ × 10½″ squares. Audition their placement on a design wall. Sew them together and press.

2. Audition your petals by placing them on the background, creating a color arrangement that is pleasing to you. That could even involve cutting another set or 2 of 10 petals if you do not like one of your sets.

Other Fabric Ideas

Below are some sample fabrics and the flowers made from them.

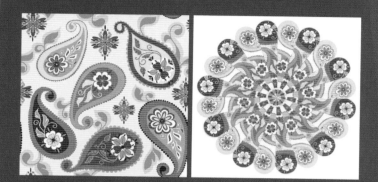

Splendor fabric by Lila Tueller Designs for Riley Blake Designs

Vintage Verona by Emily Taylor Design for Riley Blake Designs

3. Work with 2 petals at a time and begin to sew them together (refer to Sewing Dresden Petals Together, page 8). Continue adding petals until 20 are sewn into a circle. Be mindful that every other petal is the same. There will be a small hole in the center.

4. Appliqué the circle to the background squares (refer to Needle Turn Appliqué, page 8). Cut away the fabric behind the plates.

5. Make 4 yo-yo centers and sew them on the center of the Dresden plates (refer to Yo-yos, page 13).

MAKE THE BORDERS

Press after adding each border.

Border 1

1. Sew the 8 focus fabric 1″ × 20½″ strips to opposite sides of the 4 blocks.

2. Sew the 8 focus fabric 1″ × 21½″ strips to the remaining sides of the blocks.

Border 2

Make this border by sewing 3 strips together. The striped fabric D is sandwiched between 2 solid-colored fabric C strips in our quilt.

1. Sew the 26 fabric C strips end to end and cut the strip in half, forming 2 long strips.

2. Sew the 13 fabric D 1″ strips end to end.

3. Sew a fabric C strip to both sides of the fabric D strip. Press.

4. Cut 4 strips 21½″ long for sashing. Cut 4 strips 43½″ long for border 2 and set aside.

5. Cut 4 strips 56″ long for border 5 and set aside.

> **TIP** It helps to shorten the stitch length when sewing these strips. Sew with the narrower strip (fabric C) on the top and the wider strip (fabric D) on the bottom.

Center Sashing Intersection

1. Sew the 2 fabric C ¾″ × 1″ rectangles to opposite sides of the fabric D square 1″ × 1″. Press seams away from the square.

2. Sew the 2 fabric C ¾″ × 1½″ rectangles to opposite sides of the Step 1 unit. Press seams away from the square.

Assemble Center

1. Sew a 21½″ sashing strip between 2 Dresden blocks. Make 2 sets.

2. Sew the center intersection block between the 2 remaining 21½″ sashing strips.

3. Sew this sashing strip between the 2 units from Step 1.

Sashing Corners

1. Sew a fabric C ¾″ × ¾″ square to a fabric D ¾″ × 1″ rectangle.

2. Sew a fabric D 1″ × 1¼″ rectangle to the Step 1 unit.

3. Sew a fabric C ¾″ × 1¼″ rectangle to the Step 2 unit.

4. Sew a fabric C ¾″ × 1½″ rectangle to the Step 3 unit.

5. Repeat Steps 1–4 to make 8. Set aside 4 finished corners for border 5.

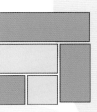

> **TIP** Note that the stripes are perpendicular to each other in these corners.

Add Border 2

1. Sew 2 of the 43½″ strips to opposite sides of the quilt.

2. Add the corners to the 2 remaining 43½″ strips and sew to the remaining sides of the quilt.

Border 3—Focus Fabric

1. Sew 2 fabric B strips 1″ × 45½″ to opposite sides of the quilt.

2. Sew 2 fabric B strips 1″ × 46½″ to the remaining sides of the quilt.

Border 4

1. Sew 2 borders 5¼″ × 46½″ to opposite sides of the quilt.

2. Sew 2 borders 5¼″ × 56″ to the remaining sides of the quilt.

Border 5

Use the pieced strips and 4 corners made and set aside in Sashing Corners.

1. Sew 2 pieced 56″ borders to opposite sides of the quilt.

2. Sew 2 corners on each end of the 2 remaining 56″ pieced borders.

3. Sew these borders to the remaining sides of the quilt.

Border 6

1. Sew 2 borders 2½″ × 58″ to opposite sides of the quilt.

2. Sew 2 borders 2½″ × 62″ to the remaining sides of the quilt.

FINISH THE QUILT

1. Layer the quilt top, batting, and backing.

2. Quilt as desired.

3. Bind using your favorite method or refer to Bonus Technique: Binding (page 100).

4. Make a label and sew it on the back of the quilt.

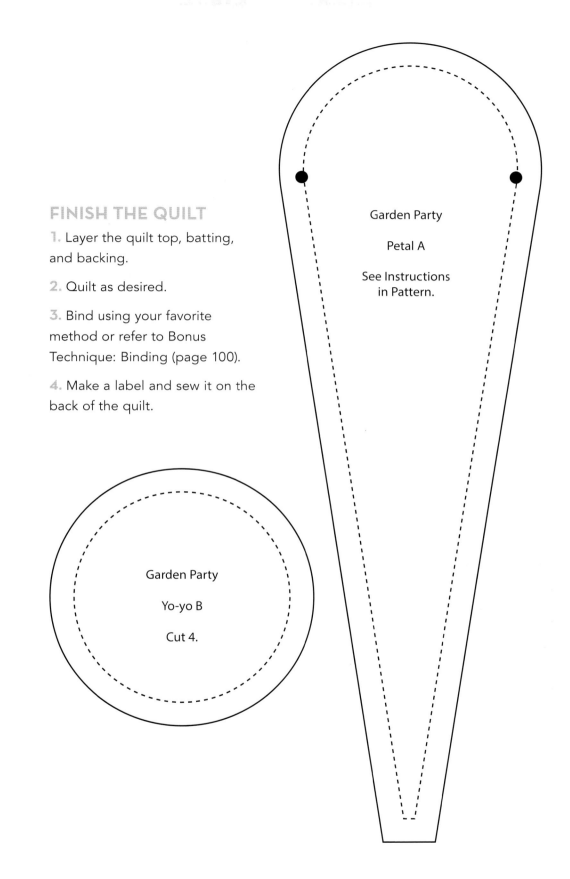

Garden Party

Petal A

See Instructions in Pattern.

Garden Party

Yo-yo B

Cut 4.

HEAT WAVE

Bring on the heat and make a bold statement with this flamboyant Dresden design! This quilt is sure to turn heads with its sizzling style and hot colors.

MATERIALS

White: 2 yards for center background

Teal P: ⅓ yard for center corners

Teal Q: ⅓ yard for center star points

Teal R: ½ yard for large petal

Teal S: ½ yard for center, border 2 stripe, and Dresden centers

Teal T: 1 yard for center and border 1 scallop

Pink U: ¼ yard for border 2 corner Dresdens

Pink V: 2¾ yards for center, medium petals, and border 2

Pink W: ½ yard for center small petals and corner Dresdens

Pink X: 1 yard for center small petals and border 2 petals

Pink Y: ½ yard for border 2 petals

Binding: ¾ yard

Backing: 4½ yards

Batting: 80″ × 80″

CUTTING

Appliqué

Make templates A through M using the *Heat Wave* patterns (pullout pages P1, P3, and P4). Refer to Making Templates (page 7) as needed.

- Cut 4 using large petal A from teal R.
- Cut 4 using medium petal B from pink V.
- Cut 4 using small petal F from pink W.
- Cut 4 using small petal F from pink X.
- Cut 1 using large center circle G from teal S.
- Cut 1 using medium center circle H from pink V.
- Cut 1 using small center circle I from teal T.
- Cut 16 using small petal J from pink U.
- Cut 16 using small petal J from pink W.
- Cut 16 using large petal K from pink X.

CUTTING *continued on page 38*

CUTTING *continued*

- Cut 16 using large petal K from pink Y.
- Cut 48 using small petal J from pink X.
- Cut 48 using small petal J from pink Y.
- Cut 16 using Dresden center L from teal S.
- Cut 8 border scallop M appliqués from teal T.

Center background

- Cut 4 teal P corner squares 8½″ × 8½″.
- Cut 4 white squares 8⅞″ × 8⅞″.
- Cut 4 teal Q squares 8⅞″ × 8⅞″.
- Cut 1 white square 16½″ × 16½″.

Border 1

Cut 4 white strips 8½″ × width of fabric, sew the strips together end to end, and cut 2 borders 8½″ × 32½″ and 2 borders 8½″ × 48½″.

Border 2 and corners

- Cut 13 pink V strips 5¾″ × width of fabric, sew 10 strips together end to end, and subcut 8 rectangles 5¾″ × 48½″.
- Subcut the 3 remaining strips into 4 squares 5¾″ × 5¾″, 4 rectangles 5¾″ × 7¼″, and 4 rectangles 5¾″ × 12½″. These rectangles are for the corners.
- Cut 7 teal S strips 2″ × width of fabric, sew 5 strips together end to end, and cut 4 strips 2″ × 48½″.
- Subcut the 2 remaining strips into 4 rectangles 2″ × 7¼″ and 4 rectangles 2″ × 5¾″. These rectangles are for the corners.

Construction

CENTER

1. Make 8 half-square triangles (refer to Half-square Triangles, page 40) using the white 8⅞″ × 8⅞″ squares and the 4 teal Q 8⅞″ × 8⅞″ squares.

2. Assemble the 8 new half-square triangles, the 4 corner squares from teal P, and the white 16½″ × 16½″ center. Press.

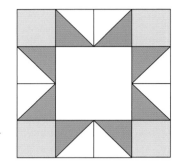

PETALS FOR THE CENTER

1. Appliqué the medium petal to the large petal (refer to Needle Turn Appliqué, page 8). For the holes C, D, and E, use the reverse appliqué method (refer to Reverse Appliqué, page 12).

2. Arrange 4 sets of small petals F, 2 sets with the pink W fabric on the left and 2 sets with the pink W fabric on the right. Sew the 4 sets of petals together at the side seam (refer to Sewing Dresden Petals Together, page 8). Press and arrange with the pointed tip at the center and the intersection of the 2 petals at the corner of the corner block.

3. Place the large petals A onto the center, following the *Heat Wave* center Dresden placement guide (pullout page P4).

4. Appliqué all the petals onto the center.

Designed by Marian Gallian and Yvette Marie Jones, made by Marian Gallian and Nancy Butler,
quilted by Kathryn Carbine • *Fabric: Henna by Beth Studley for Makower UK*

5. Make the 3 appliqué concentric centers using Perfect Circles (page 13). Appliqué the small circle to the medium circle, and then the medium circle to the large circle, before appliquéing to the center of the petals.

Half-Square Triangles

When you have large quantities of half-square triangles to make, the work goes faster using an assembly line approach—preparing and doing one step and moving on to the next step.

1. Start with 2 contrasting fabrics. To determine how big to cut the starting squares, start with the measurement of the finished half-square triangle and add 7/8″ to that. For example, to make 2 finished 3″ half-square triangles, cut 2 squares 3⅞″. If you need only 1 half-square triangle, put the leftover in an orphan square box or make a label out of it.

3. Stitch a scant ¼″ to the right and left of the drawn diagonal line. Using a scant ¼″ seam allowance allows for the space that is taken up when you fold back the fabric.

4. Cut the 2 triangles apart on the drawn line. You now have 2 half-square triangles. Lightly press the square open using an up-and-down motion. Using a back-and-forth ironing motion will distort the square.

2. Place the 2 squares right sides together. Use a straight edge to draw a pencil line diagonally across the back of the lightest color fabric. If both fabrics are dark, use a white or yellow pencil.

The fabric is easier to work with if you press the squares together at this point and pin them together after pressing.

Your block should measure the size of your finished half-square triangle with ¼″ seam allowances on all 4 sides. In the example above, the square should be 3″ × 3″ with a ¼″ seam allowance on all 4 sides, or 3½″ × 3½″ square.

5. Trim your squares, if needed.

MAKE THE BORDERS

Press after adding each border.

Border 1

1. Sew 2 borders 8½″ × 32½″ to either side of the center.

2. Sew 2 borders 8½″ × 48½″ to the opposite sides of the center.

3. Appliqué 2 teal T scallops to each side of the quilt.

Border 2 Corners

1. Arrange the pieces as shown and sew together in numerical order.

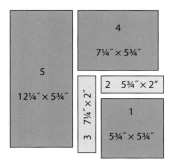

2. Make 4 small Dresdens from the 16 blue U and 16 pink W petals.

3. Make 4 larger Dresdens from the 16 pink X and 16 pink Y petals. Press all the petals using the *Heat Wave* corner Dresden placement and pressing guide (pullout page P3). Refer to Pressing and Blocking (page 12).

4. Make 16 teal S centers using Perfect Circles (page 13). Appliqué teal centers to the center of the 4 small Dresdens. Set aside 12 centers for border 2.

5. Appliqué the small Dresdens to the larger ones.

6. Appliqué the large Dresdens to the center of each corner.

Border 2

1. Sew a pink border strip to either side of a teal strip to make 4 border strips.

2. Make 12 small Dresdens from the 48 pink X and 48 pink Y and the 12 teal S centers, set aside above.

3. Center 1 small Dresden on the center of each border. Measure 10″ from the ends of each border and center the other small Dresdens on the marks. Appliqué all.

4. Sew 2 borders to opposite sides of the quilt. Sew the corner blocks to each end of the remaining 2 strips. Sew the borders to the quilt.

FINISH THE QUILT

1. Layer the quilt top, batting, and backing.

2. Quilt as desired.

3. Bind using your favorite method or refer to Bonus Technique: Binding (page 100).

4. Make a label and sew it on the back of the quilt.

ITALIAN ICE

I loved to walk to the old soda shoppe with my best friend and sit on those tall stools that spin around and order an Italian soda. We would sip and spin in this quaint old store that had a vintage tile floor with striking geometric patterns and flower boxes just outside the window, while enjoying our freedom from school.

MATERIALS

White: ⅝ yard

Gray: ¼ yard

Gray print: ⅜ yard

Black: 4 yards

Gray-and-white chevron: ¼ yard

Yellow-and-gray chevron: ⅝ yard

Yellow: 1 yard

Yellow print: ¾ yard

Small Dresden fans: ⅛ yard each of 8 colors

Large Dresden fans: ¼ yard each of 8 colors

Binding: ¾ yard

Backing: 4½ yards

Batting: 80″ × 80″

CUTTING

Appliqué

Make templates A through H using the *Italian Ice* patterns (pages 47–49). Refer to Making Templates (page 7) as needed.

- Cut 64 small petals A, 8 from each of 8 different fabrics.
- Cut 16 small quarter-circles B from black.
- Cut 224 medium triangles C from black.

CUTTING *continued on page 44*

Skill level: confident beginner

Finished quilt: 72" × 72"

Finished blocks: 6" × 6" and 7" × 7"

CUTTING *continued*

- Cut 56 large triangles D from yellow print.
- Cut 56 large triangles D from yellow.
- Cut 32 small triangles E from yellow.
- Cut 32 small triangles E from black.
- Cut 80 large petals F, 10 from each of 8 different fabrics.
- Cut 4 large quarter-circles G from gray.
- Cut 8 semicircles H from gray.

Center

- Cut 16 white squares 6½″ × 6½″.

Sashing and sashing corners

- Cut 24 gray sashing strips 1″ × 6½″.
- Cut 9 black sashing corners 1″ × 1″.

Border 1

- Cut 2 black strips 1″ × 26″.
- Cut 2 black strips 1″ × 27″.

Border 2

- Cut 2 gray-and-white chevron strips 1¼″ × 27″.
- Cut 2 gray-and-white chevron strips 1¼″ × 28½″.

Border 3

- Cut 20 black squares 7½″ × 7½″.

Border 4

- Cut 5 gray print strips 1¾″ × width of fabric, sew the strips together end to end, and cut 2 strips 1¾″ × 42½″ and 2 strips 1¾″ × 45″.

Border 5

- Cut 6 black strips 8¼″ × width of fabric, sew the 6 strips together end to end, and cut 2 strips 8¼″ × 45″ and 2 strips 8¼″ × 60½″.

Border 6

- Cut 7 yellow-and-gray chevron strips 2½″ × width of fabric, sew 6 strips together end to end, and cut 4 border strips 2½″ × 56″.
- From the remaining strip, subcut 12 squares 2½″ × 2½″.
- Cut 1 black strip 2½″ × width of fabric; subcut 8 rectangles 2½″ × 4½″ and 4 squares 4½″ × 4½″.

Construction

Press after adding each border.

SEW TOGETHER THE SMALL PETALS

1. Use a design wall to arrange your Dresden pieces in a pleasing arrangement. Make 4 sets of 4 quarter-circles, 16 total (refer to Sewing Dresden Petals Together, page 8).

2. Press using the *Italian Ice* 6″ Dresden pressing guide (page 48). Refer to Pressing and Blocking (page 12).

Designed by Marian Gallian, made by Marian Gallian and Nancy Butler, quilted by Kathy Carbine
Fabric: Modern Folkloric by Makower UK

Italian Ice

ASSEMBLE THE SMALL BLOCKS

1. Appliqué the petal sets to the 6½″ × 6½″ squares (refer to Needle Turn Appliqué, page 8). Appliqué the black small centers in place. Press.

2. Arrange the 24 gray sashing strips and the 9 sashing corners. Sew the blocks, sashing strips, and corners together into rows and then sew the rows together.

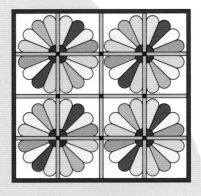

MAKE THE BORDERS

Border 1

1. Sew 2 black strips 1″ × 26″ to opposite sides of the center.

2. Sew 2 black strips 1″ × 27″ to the remaining sides of the center.

Border 2

1. Sew 2 gray-and-white chevron strips 1¼″ × 27″ to opposite sides of the center.

2. Sew 2 gray-and-white chevron strips 1¼″ × 28½″ to the remaining sides of the center.

Border 3

Refer to Sew Together the Small Petals (page 44) as needed, using large petal F, large quarter-circle G, and Italian Ice 7″ Dresden pressing guide (page 49).

1. Use a design wall to arrange the Dresden petals in a pleasing arrangement. Make 2 sets of 10 quarter-circles, 20 total.

2. Appliqué the petal sets to the squares.

3. Appliqué the 20 large gray quarter-circles and semicircles.

4. Arrange the blocks and sew them into rows and then sew the rows to the quilt top. Press.

Border 4

1. Sew 2 strips 1¾″ × 42½″ to opposite sides of the center.

2. Sew 2 strips 1¾″ × 45″ to the remaining sides of the center.

Border 5

1. Sew 2 strips 8¼″ × 45″ to opposite sides of the center.

2. Sew 2 strips 8¼″ × 60½″ to the remaining sides of the center.

Border 6

1. Make 112 yellow Flying Geese blocks using 56 yellow print triangles D, 56 yellow triangles D, and 224 black corner triangles C.

2. Make 16 quarter-square triangles from 32 yellow triangles E and 32 black triangles E.

3. Refer to the layout and sew 4 borders using the Flying Geese from Step 1 (Border 6) on the previous page, 8 of the quarter-square triangles from Step 2 (Border 6) on the previous page, and the pieces below:

- 4 yellow-and-gray chevron strips 2½˝ × 56˝
- 8 black 2½˝ × 4½˝ strips

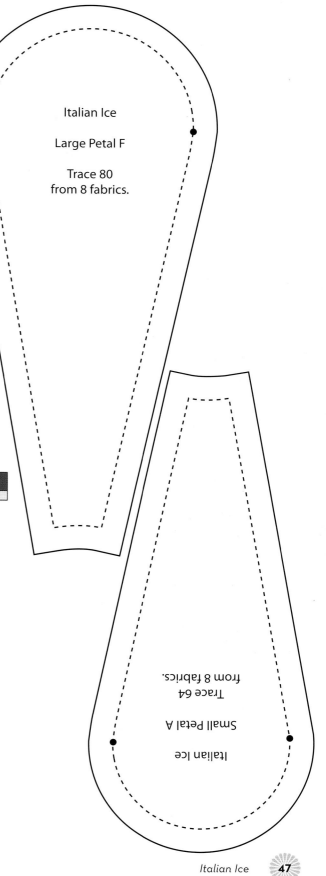

4. Sew 2 borders to opposite sides of the quilt.

5. Refer to the layout and sew the pieces below to the 2 remaining strips, with the remaining 8 quarter-square triangles from Step 2:

- 4 black 4½˝ × 4½˝ squares
- 12 yellow-and-gray chevron squares 2½˝ × 2½˝

6. Sew the borders to the top and bottom of the quilt.

FINISH THE QUILT

1. Layer the quilt top, batting, and backing.

2. Quilt as desired.

3. Bind using your favorite method or refer to Bonus Technique: Binding (page 100).

4. Make a label and sew it on the back of the quilt.

Italian Ice

Large Petal F

Trace 80
from 8 fabrics.

Trace 64
from 8 fabrics.

Small Petal A

Italian Ice

Italian Ice
Large
Quarter-circle G
Trace 4.

Italian Ice
Large Triangle D
Trace 112
(56 from yellow
and 56 from
yellow print).

Italian Ice
Medium Triangle C
Trace 244.

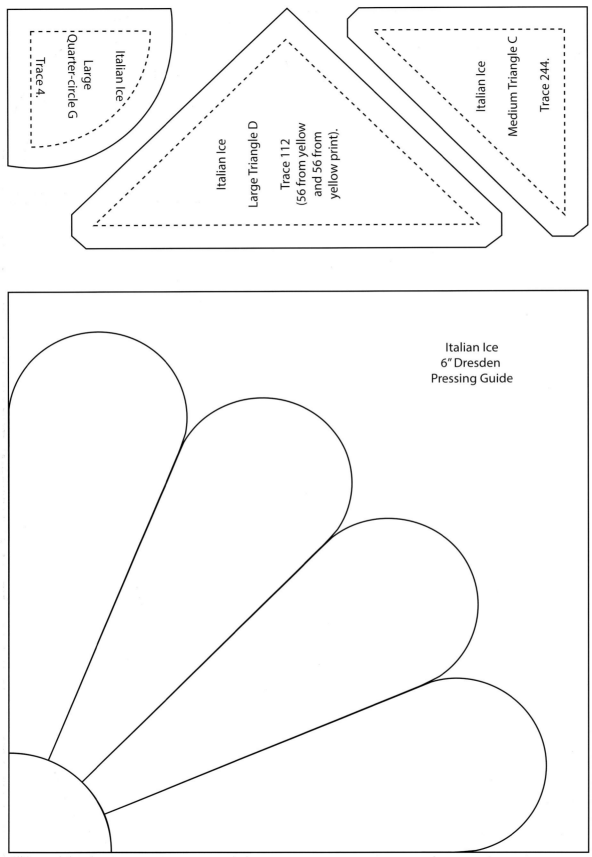

Italian Ice
6" Dresden
Pressing Guide

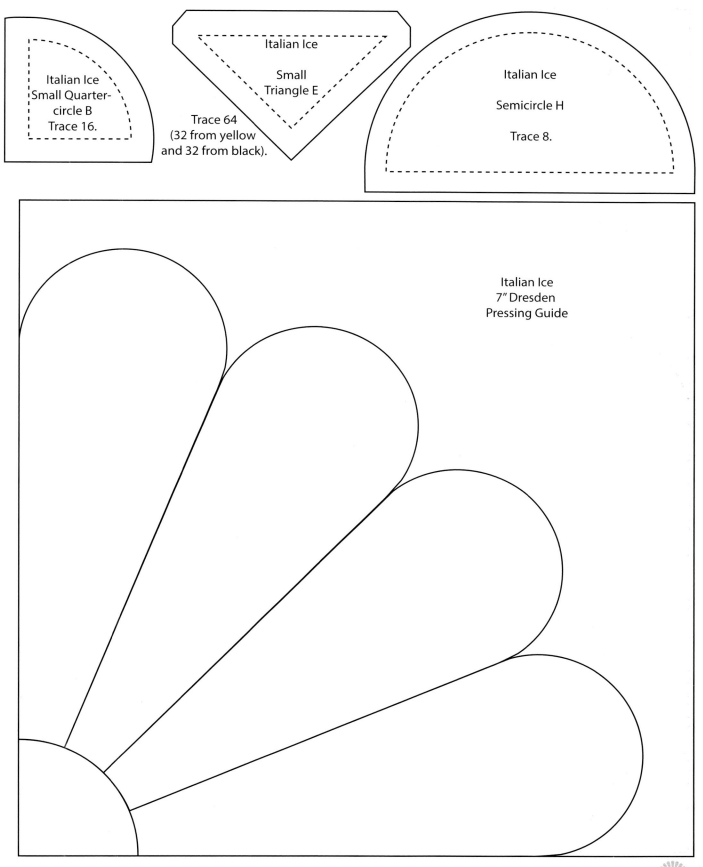

Italian Ice
Small Quarter-
circle B
Trace 16.

Italian Ice

Small
Triangle E

Trace 64
(32 from yellow
and 32 from black).

Italian Ice

Semicircle H

Trace 8.

Italian Ice
7" Dresden
Pressing Guide

HOLLY JOLLY

Finished blocks: 8″ × 8″ and 10″ × 10″

Finished quilt: 62½″ × 62½″

Skill level: confident beginner

We are celebrating Christmas in July with this holiday-themed version of the quilt. This quilt was made to express the joy of the Christmas season in a traditional quilt.

MATERIALS

White: 1⅛ yards for Dresden background

Striped fabric: ¼ yard for sashing

Black: ¼ yard for border 1 and sashing corners

Border 2: ¼ yard

Border 3: ⅜ yard

Border 4: 1¾ yards

Border 5: ⅓ yard

Dresden centers: ¼ yard

Small Dresden petals: ⅛ yard each of 16 colors

Large Dresden petals: ½ yard each of 4 colors

Binding: ⅝ yard

Backing: 4 yards

Batting: 70″ × 70″

Designed and made by Marian Gallian, quilted by Kathy Carbine
Fabrics: Holly Jolly by Jen Allyson for Riley Blake Designs

CUTTING

Appliqué

Make templates A, B, C, D, and E using the *Holly Jolly* patterns (page 53). Refer to Making Templates (page 7) as needed.

Center (small Dresden fan blocks)

- Cut 64 small petals A, 4 petals from each of 16 fabrics.
- Cut 16 small quarter-circles B.

Border 4 (large Dresden fan blocks)

- Cut 20 large petals C from each of 4 colorways.
- Cut 4 large quarter-circles D.
- Cut 8 large semicircles E.

Center (small Dresden fan blocks)

- Cut 16 white squares 8½″ × 8½″.
- Cut 24 striped sashing strips 1″ × 8½″.
- Cut 9 black sashing corners 1″ × 1″.

Border 1

- Cut 2 black strips 1″ × 34″.
- Cut 2 black strips 1″ × 35″.

Border 2

- Cut 2 strips 1½″ × 35″.
- Cut 2 strips 1½″ × 37″.

Border 3

- Cut 2 strips 2¼″ × 37″.
- Cut 2 strips 2¼″ × 40½″.

Border 4 (large Dresden fan blocks)

- Cut 20 squares 10½″ × 10½″.

Border 5

- Cut 6 strips 1½″ × width of fabric, sew the strips together end to end, and cut 2 borders 1½″ × 60½″ and 2 borders 1½″ × 62½″.

Construction

Press after adding each border. The construction of this quilt is similar to Italian Ice (page 42). Refer back to that project if needed.

SEW TOGETHER THE SMALL PETALS

Note: Each Dresden plate in the center will have 16 different fabrics randomly placed.

Use a design wall to arrange your Dresden pieces in a pleasing arrangement. Make 4 sets of 4 quarter-circles, 16 total (refer to Sewing Dresden Petals Together, page 8).

ASSEMBLE THE SMALL BLOCKS

1. Appliqué the petal sets to the 8½″ × 8½″ squares (refer to Needle Turn Appliqué, page 8). Appliqué the quarter-circles in place. Press.

2. Arrange the 24 sashing strips and the 9 sashing corners with the Dresden blocks. Sew the blocks, sashing strips, and corners into rows and then sew rows together.

MAKE THE BORDERS

Border 1

1. Sew 2 black 1″ × 34″ strips to opposite sides of the center.

2. Sew 2 black 1″ × 35″ strips to the remaining sides of the center.

Border 2

1. Sew 2 border 2 strips 1½″ × 35″ to opposite sides of the center.

2. Sew 2 border 2 strips 1½″ × 37″ to the remaining sides of the center.

Border 3

1. Sew 2 border 3 strips 2¼″ × 37″ to opposite sides of the center.

2. Sew 2 border 3 strips 2¼″ × 40½″ to the remaining sides of the center.

Border 4

1. Use a design wall to place the Dresden petals in a pleasing arrangement. Make 20 identical sets of 4 quarter-circles (refer to Sew Together the Small Petals, page 44, and Assemble the Small Blocks, page 46, from *Italian Ice* as needed).

2. Appliqué the petal sets to the 10½″ × 10½″ squares.

3. Arrange the blocks and sew them into rows and then sew the rows to the quilt top. Press.

4. Appliqué the 20 quarter-circles and semicircles in place.

Border 5

1. Sew 2 borders 1½″ × 60½″ to opposite sides of the center.

2. Sew 2 borders 1½″ × 62½″ to the remaining sides of the center.

FINISH THE QUILT

1. Layer the quilt top, batting, and backing.

2. Quilt as desired.

3. Bind using your favorite method or refer to Bonus Technique: Binding (page 100).

4. Make a label and sew it on the back of the quilt.

Quilt assembly

Holly Jolly

Large Quarter-circle D

Trace 4.

Holly Jolly

Small Quarter-circle B

Trace 16.

Holly Jolly

Large Petal C

Trace 80
from 4 fabrics.

Holly Jolly

Small Petal A

Trace 64
from 16 fabrics.

Holly Jolly

Large Semicircle E

Trace 8.

LEMONADE AND LACE

We started with visions of lemonade stands and bright, sunny summer days, and then we took some liberties with the Dresden petal, creating an eyelet look that resulted in a creative design layout. We finished by adding delicate eyelet holes and sweet scallops to the border.

MATERIALS

Petals: Approximately 2 yards total of 12 or more diversified fabrics to make the quilt more interesting

Background: 4 yards

Bias Binding: 1 yard (See Continuous Bias Binding, page 101.)

Backing: 4 yards

Batting: 72″ × 72″

CUTTING

Petals: Cut 144 rectangles 3½″ × 5″.

Background squares: Cut 36 squares 8½″ × 8½″.

Border 1: Cut 6 strips 8½″ × width of fabric.

Bias binding: Cut 1 square 30″ × 30″.

Construction

MAKE TEMPLATES A AND B

1. Make templates A and B using the *Lemonade and Lace* petal patterns A and B (pullout page P3). Refer to Making Templates (page 7) as needed.

2. Cut out both notches on template A and clip the notch lines on template B.

3. Cut out the center circles on the templates. Be sure you cut very smooth, perfect circles for best results.

Skill level:
intermediate

Finished quilt:
64½" × 64½"

Finished block:
8" × 8"

PREPARE THE PETALS

1. Place template A on the right side of a 3½″ × 5″ piece of petal fabric and trace around the template with a mechanical pencil. Be sure to include the notches and center hole when tracing. *Figure A*

2. Carefully cut out the petals on the drawn line. *Do not cut out the notches or the inner circle. Figure B*

3. Turn the petal wrong side up and center template B on it. Pencil in the notches in the seam allowance. *Figure C*

4. Turn the petal right side up and place template B on it, matching the notches. Trace around the top arc of the petal from notch to notch and trace the center circle. On the bottom edge, trace the seam allowance arc. *Figures D & E*

5. Cut out the inside of the circle, leaving approximately a ¼″ seam allowance.

TIP The trick to a perfect circle is to fold the fabric in half at the center of the circle and cut a very small slit. Cut out the circle, leaving a ¼″ seam allowance.

Using the tip of small, sharp embroidery scissors, carefully clip the fabric to within 1–3 threads of the drawn line. Make lots of clips to create a smoother appliquéd circle (refer to Stitching Concave Curves, page 10, and Reverse Appliqué, page 12).

(A)

(B)

(C)

(D)

(E)

Designed by Marian Gallian and Yvette Jones, made by Marian Gallian, quilted by Kathryn Carbine • *Fabric: Make it scrappy, using lots of shades of yellow on the petals with a creamy yellow background fabric.*

ASSEMBLE THE BLOCKS

1. Place 2 randomly selected petals right sides together and sew. Add 2 more petals to make a 4-petal set (refer to Sewing Dresden Petals Together, page 8). Make 36 sets of 4 petals.

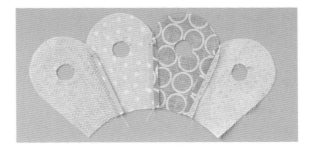

2. Place each 4-petal set on a background square so that the bottom raw edge of the petals are 4″ from the corner. This is important in making the blocks appear to have a seamless curve. Baste or pin the petals to the background.

3. Appliqué the top edge of the petals, turning under at the drawn line (refer to Needle Turn Appliqué, page 8). Next, appliqué the ¼″ seam on the bottom edge to the background, turning under at the drawn line. The edge that is turned under should be 4¼″ from the unfinished corner. Reverse appliqué the circles (refer to Reverse Appliqué, page 12).

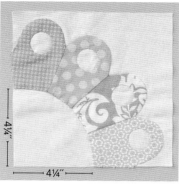

TIP When you needle-turn appliqué the center circle to the background, use your needle to create a sweeping motion, and sweep the clipped edges under a few at a time as you sew. If you have done your preparation correctly, the circle will appear perfectly like magic. Use small stitches when appliquéing the inside circle.

CONSTRUCT THE CENTER

1. Arrange the 36 appliquéd squares according to the quilt assembly diagram on the next page.

2. Sew the blocks together. Be accurate in joining the blocks together to match the sides as pictured.

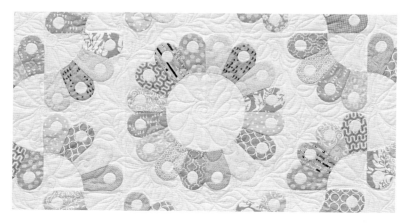

MAKE THE BORDER

1. Sew the 8½″ × 48½″ strips to the right and left sides of the quilt top.

2. Sew the 8½″ × 64½″ strips to the top and bottom of the quilt top. *Figure A*

3. Make the *Lemonade and Lace* corner template (pullout page P3) and trace the template on all 4 corners of the quilt top. Be sure to mark the circles very carefully. Do not cut out the circles or the edge of the border. *Figure B*

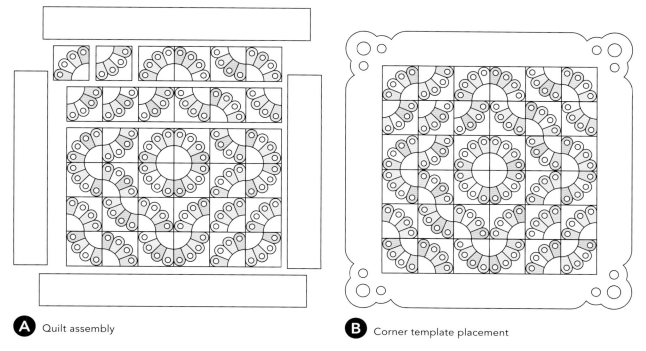

A Quilt assembly

B Corner template placement

FINISH THE QUILT

1. Layer the quilt top, batting, and backing.

2. Quilt as desired, making sure you don't quilt closer than ¼˝ to the border circles; if you are sending the quilt out for quilting, be sure to include this instruction. Trim the corners after quilting.

MAKING THE BORDER CIRCLES

TIP **Make some practice holes using 2 pieces of scrap fabric and a piece of batting. Draw the inner and outer circles and proceed as directed in the instructions that follow.**

1. Draw an inner circle with a mechanical pencil approximately ¼˝ inside the outer circle.

2. Cut out the top layer of the fabric and batting along the inner circle. Do not cut out the bottom layer of fabric.

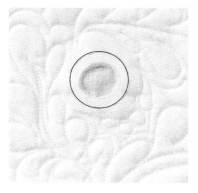

3. Trim only the batting back an additional ¼″ from the hole. Clip the seam allowance of the top layer of fabric to the outer circle. *Figure A*

4. Sweep the clipped seam allowance under the batting and baste all 3 layers together. (Basting is shown in red thread.) *Figure B*

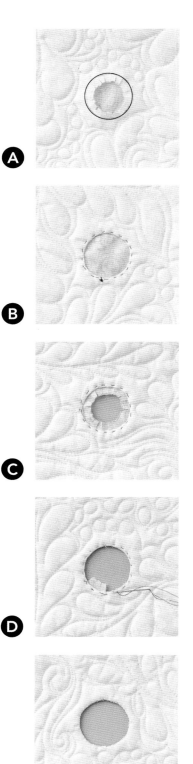

 Basting helps to hold the shape and make smooth curves while you are working with bias edges that can get stretched out of shape. Don't skip this step!

5. Cut a hole in the bottom layer, leaving a ¼″ seam allowance. Clip the curve. *Figure C*

6. Release the basting stitches a couple of stitches at a time, tuck under the bottom seam allowance, and rebaste. (Rebasting is shown with green thread.) *Figure D*

7. Use small whipstitches or ladder stitches to hand stitch the hole closed. (Blue thread is used for purposes of this photo only.) The thread should match the background fabric. *Figure E*

Ladder Stitch

A ladder stitch is good to use when sewing openings closed.

Right side of fabric
Start knot between the layers of fabric.
Folded edge
5 4 1
3 2
Machine seam

BIND AND LABEL

1. Bind using bias strips (refer to Continuous Bias Binding, page 101).

2. Make a label and sew it on the back of the quilt.

PINK LEMONADE AND LACE PILLOW

Finished block: 10" × 10"

Finished pillow: 20" × 20"

Skill level: intermediate

MATERIALS

Petals: 16 different fabric scraps at least 3½" × 5"

Background: 4 different squares at least 10¾" × 10¾".

Quilt backing: ⅞ yard

Pillow back: ⅝ yard

Batting: 1 square 28" × 28"

Pillow form: 20" × 20"

CUTTING

Petals: Cut 1 rectangle 3½" × 5" from each of the 16 petal fabrics.

Background squares: Cut 4 background fabric squares 10¾" × 10¾".

Quilt backing: Cut 1 square 28" × 28".

Pillow back: Cut 1 square 21" × 21".

Designed and made by Marian Gallian, quilted by Kathryn Carbine • *Fabric: Make it scrappy using shades of pink on a pieced taupe background.*

Construction

1. Use the same templates and techniques from the *Lemonade and Lace* quilt (page 54).

2. Mark each 10¾" × 10¾" square 4¼" up adjoining sides and line up the 4 petal sets with these marks as in *Lemonade and Lace*; proceed to finish the 4 blocks as instructed.

3. Arrange the 4 appliquéd squares to form a circle. Press the seam allowances of the blocks so they will nest together. Sew the blocks together.

PILLOW ASSEMBLY

1. Layer the pillow top, batting, and quilt backing.

2. Quilt as desired.

3. To complete the pillow, follow the instructions for Cotton Candy Pillow Assembly (page 26).

FERRIS WHEEL

Did you ever get on the Ferris wheel with your sweetheart, ride to the top where you stop, and steal a kiss while overlooking the sparkling lights of the fair below? This quilt boasts a center medallion of art deco–inspired flowers arranged like the spokes of a Ferris wheel and surrounded by traditional Dresdens.

MATERIALS

Pink and white: ¼ yard

Mini pink hearts: ¼ yard

Green and white: ¼ yard

Mini green hearts: ½ yard

Solid green: ¾ yard

Gray-on-gray: 1½ yards

Pink-on-pink: 1 yard

Cream: 1⅛ yards

Pink stripe: 1¾ yards
(for lengthwise stripe)

Binding: ½ yard

Backing: 3¾ yards

Batting: 67″ × 67″

CUTTING

Appliqué

Make templates A through L using the *Ferris Wheel* patterns (pullout pages P1–P3). Refer to Making Templates (page 7) as needed.

- Cut 12 large petals A from pink and white.
- Cut 12 large petals A from mini pink hearts.
- Cut 24 small petals B from green and white.
- Cut 24 small petals B from mini green hearts.
- Cut 4 quarter-circles C from solid green.
- Cut 4 semicircles D from solid green.
- Cut 4 small flowers E from gray-on-gray.
- Cut 4 medium flowers F from solid green.

CUTTING continued on page 64

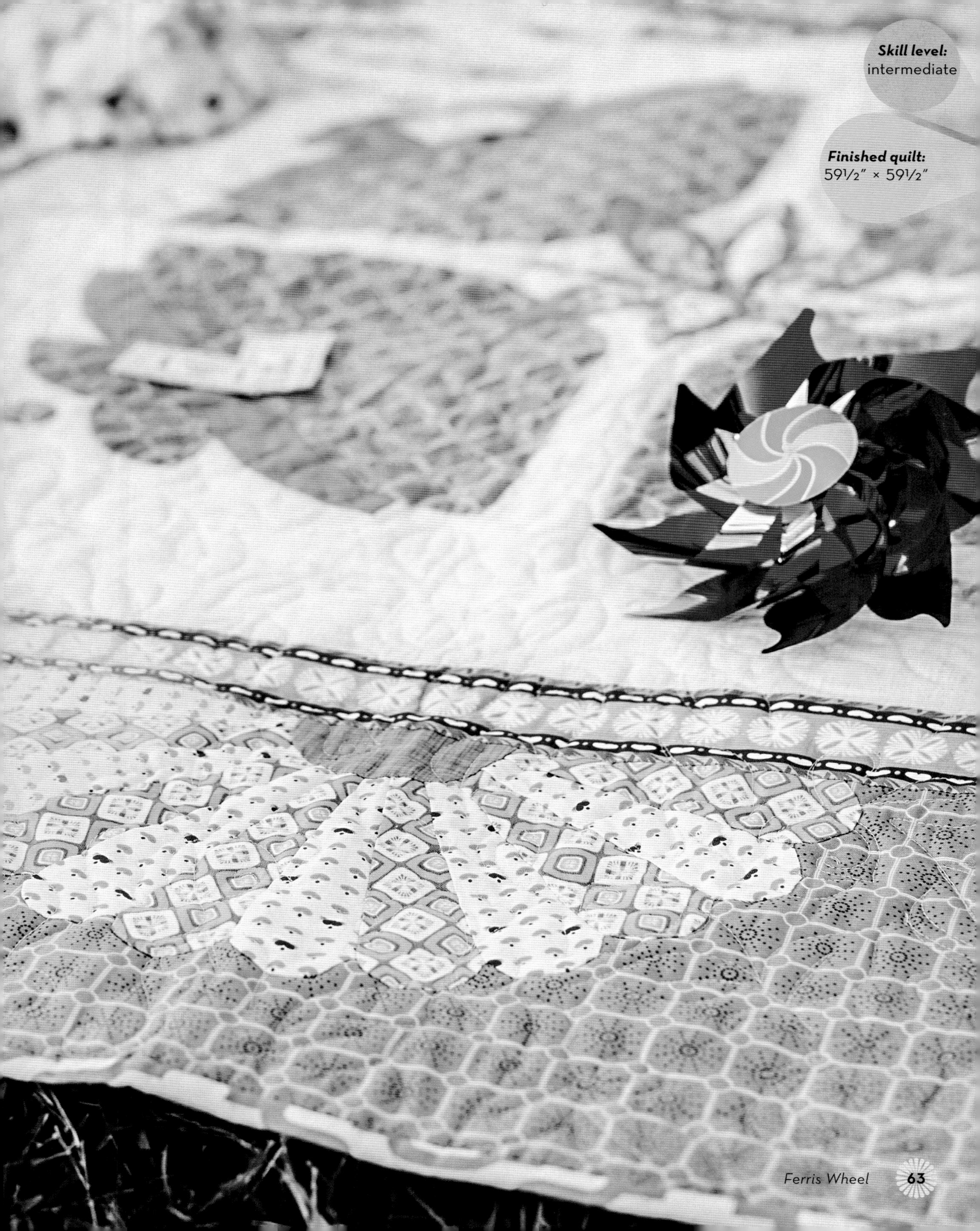

Skill level: intermediate

Finished quilt: 59½" × 59½"

CUTTING *continued*

- Cut 4 large flowers G from pink-on-pink.
- Cut 4 flowers dots H from pink-on-pink.
- Cut 12 corner leaves I from solid green.
- Cut 12 corner leaves J from mini green hearts.
- Cut 4 center leaves K from pink-on-pink and 4 from solid green.
- Cut 4 center leaves L from green and white and 4 from mini green hearts.

Background

- Cut 1 cream square 35½″ × 35½″.

Border 2

- Fussy cut 2 pink stripe strips 2½″ × 35½″.
- Fussy cut 2 pink stripe strips 2½″ × 59½″.
- Fussy cut 4 stripe strips 2½″ × 10½″.

Border 3

- Cut 4 gray-on-gray pieces 10½″ × 35½″.
- Cut 4 pink-on-pink squares 10½″ × 10½″.

Construction

CENTER

1. Sew the pink petals into 4 quarter-fans (refer to Sewing Dresden Petals Together, page 8). Press and block using the *Ferris Wheel* large quarter-circle Dresden pressing guide (pullout page P1). Refer to Pressing and Blocking (page 12).

2. Appliqué the quarter-fans to the 4 corners of the cream center (refer to Needle Turn Appliqué, page 8, as needed).

3. Center the green quarter-circle centers C and appliqué.

4. Finger-press the cream center background into 4 quadrants horizontally and vertically, and then again diagonally. Use these pressed lines along with the *Ferris Wheel* flower appliqué placement guide (pullout page P1) to line up the flower appliqué shapes E, F, G, and H on the quilt as shown in the photo on the next page; refer to Making Dresden Blocks (page 8) as needed.

5. Appliqué the flowers in place.

6. Place appliqué shapes K and L on the cream square using the *Ferris Wheel* center leaves appliqué placement guide (pullout page P1) and folded lines.

7. Appliqué the motifs in place.

Designed by Yvette Marie Jones, made by Marian Gallian and Nancy Butler, quilted by Kathryn Carbine
Fabric: Fontaine by Yvette Marie Jones of Vetmari for P&B Textiles

GRAY BORDERS

1. Fold the gray rectangles in half and finger-press to find the center.

2. Sew the green petals into half-fans. Block and press using the *Ferris Wheel* border quarter-circle Dresden pressing guide (pullout page P2).

3. Center and appliqué the half-fans onto the border rectangles.

4. Appliqué the green semicircle centers D.

CORNERS

1. Place appliqué shapes I and J on the 4 pink squares using the *Ferris Wheel* corner leaves appliqué placement guide (pullout page P1).

2. Appliqué the leaves in layers.

CORNERS

1. Sew 1 fussy-cut 2½″ × 10½″ stripe strip to each end of 2 gray-on-gray borders.

2. Sew 1 corner to each end of these borders.

3. Sew 2 fussy cut 2½″ × 35½″ stripe strips to opposite sides of the center.

4. Sew 2 gray-on-gray border pieces to the same sides as in Step 3.

5. Sew 2 fussy-cut 2½″ × 59½″ stripe strips to the sides of the center unit.

6. Sew the borders from Step 2 to the center unit.

FINISH THE QUILT

1. Layer the quilt top, batting, and backing.

2. Quilt as desired.

3. Bind using your favorite method or refer to Bonus Technique: Binding (page 100).

4. Make a label and sew it on the back of the quilt.

BONUS PROJECT:
CAROUSEL TABLE TOPPER

MATERIALS

Main green print: 1½ yards for center and bias binding

Green: ¼ yard   **Gray:** 1⅛ yards

Cream: ⅛ yard   **Backing:** 1¼ yards

Red violet: ½ yard   **Batting:** 44″ × 44″

CUTTING

Appliqués

Make templates E through L using the *Ferris Wheel* patterns (pullout pages P1–P3). Refer to Making Templates (page 7) as needed.

- Cut 4 small flowers E from green.
- Cut 4 medium flowers F from red violet.
- Cut 4 large flowers G from main green print.
- Cut 4 flower dots H from red violet.
- Cut 4 corner leaves I from red violet.
- Cut 4 corner leaves J from cream.
- Cut 4 center leaves K from green.
- Cut 4 center leaves L from red violet.

Background

- Cut 1 gray square 36½″ × 36½″.

Bias Binding

- Cut 1 square 25″ × 25″ from main green print.

Finished quilt: 36½″ × 36½″

Skill level: confident beginner

Designed by Yvette Marie Jones, made by Nancy Butler, quilted by Kathryn Carbine • *Fabrics: Fontaine by Yvette Marie Jones of Vetmari for P&B Textiles*

Construction

Use the Center instructions (page 64) from *Ferris Wheel* and use the *Lemonade and Lace* corner pattern (pullout page P3) for the border.

FINISH THE QUILT

1. Layer the quilt top, batting, and backing.

2. Quilt as desired.

3. Bind using bias strips. Refer to Continuous Bias Binding (page 101).

4. Make a label and sew it on the back of the quilt.

LILY PAD

Searching for frogs at the edge of a pond dotted with lily pads is a favorite summer pastime for children. The modern, geometric Dresdens in this quilt remind us of those lily pads floating in the pond.

MATERIALS

Light green: 1⅛ yards

Dark green plaid: 1⅛ yards

White plaid: ¼ yard

Medium green: ⅜ yard

Blue-green print: ⅔ yard

Background: 3½ yards

Binding: ⅝ yard

Backing: 3¾ yards

Batting: 68″ × 68″

Paper-backed fusible web: 2 yards

CUTTING

Appliqué

Make templates A, B, C, D, and E using the *Lily Pad* patterns (pullout pages P1 and P2). Refer to Making Templates (page 7) as needed.

Wedges, Triangles, and Squares

- Light green: Cut 5 strips 7″ × width of fabric. Use wedge A to cut 36 wedges.

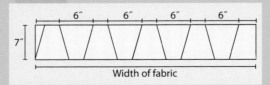

- Dark green plaid: Cut 5 strips 7″ × width of fabric. Use wedge A to cut 36 wedges.

- Medium green: Cut 2 strips 5½″ × width of fabric. Use triangle D to cut 20 triangles.

Circles

- Blue-green print: Cut 4 circles B and 4 semicircles C, adding ½″ extra outside the curved edges.

White plaid

- Cut 1 strip 6″ × width of fabric; subcut 3 squares 6″ × 6″ and 2 triangles E.

Background fabric

- Cut 2 strips 30½″ × 60½″.

Designed by Yvette Marie Jones, made by
Nancy Butler, quilted by Kathryn Carbine
*Fabric: Modern Meadow in the Berry
colorway by Joel Dewberry*

Construction

PREPARE FUSIBLE WEB

1. Trace 4 circles B and
4 semicircles C onto the paper
side of the fusible web.

2. Cut out the circles, leaving
a ¼˝ cutting allowance on the
outside. Also trim away the
inside of the circles, leaving
½˝. This will leave your
finished quilt more pliable.

MAKE THE PETAL UNITS

1. Alternate sewing the 6 light green and 6 dark green plaid
wedges to form 4 lily pads.

2. Make the
4 lily pad
halves by
sewing 3 light
green and
3 dark green
plaid wedges
together.

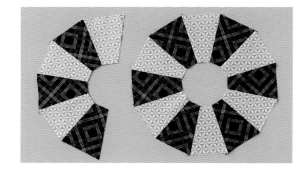

3. Center and fuse the fusible web pieces to the circles B and
the semicircles C, following the manufacturer's instructions.

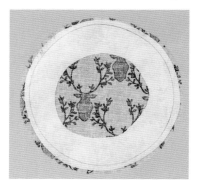

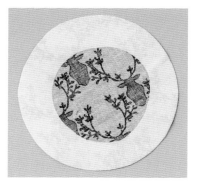

Designed by Yvette Marie Jones, made by Marian Gallian and Nancy Butler, quilted by
Kathryn Carbine • *Fabric: Rustique by Emily Herrick for Michael Miller Fabrics*

Lily Pad

4. Fold the circles into quarters and finger-press. If using directional fabric, watch your alignment when folding the circles. Align the circles with the vertical and horizontal lines on the lily pad. Fold the semicircles in half to align with the center seam on the lily pad half.

5. Fuse the circles and semicircles in place and finish the fused appliqué with a blanket stitch or a ⅛″ line stitched along the raw edge.

TIP The semi-circle needs extra care. Pin the lily pad half to the ironing surface. Measure to make sure the distance left open is 7¼″. Then place semi-circle B, aligning the straight edges and the fold with the center seam. Semicircle B will overlap the inner edges of the lily pad half.

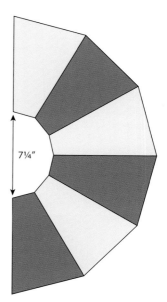

7¼″

SEW TOGETHER THE SQUARE UNITS

1. Finger-press the 6″ × 6″ squares into diagonal quarters.

2. Align a triangle D on 1 side of a square, with the tip resting on the folded line.

3. Sew and press.

4. Repeat for all 3 remaining triangles. Make 3 units.

SEW THE BACKGROUND

Sew the 2 background 30½˝ × 60½˝ strips together to create a 60½˝ × 60½˝ background square.

ASSEMBLE THE UNITS

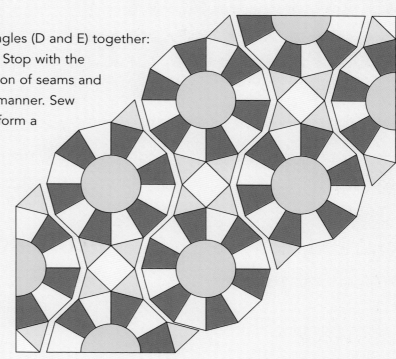

1. Sew the units and extra triangles (D and E) together: Begin sewing in a straight line. Stop with the needle down at each intersection of seams and pivot. Continue sewing in this manner. Sew the large sections together to form a large diagonal appliqué.

2. Pin and baste the pieced unit to the background. Appliqué it to the background (refer to Needle Turn Appliqué, page 8). If desired, cut away the background fabric behind the appliqué, leaving a ½˝ seam allowance.

FINISH THE QUILT

1. Layer the quilt top, batting, and backing.

2. Quilt as desired.

3. Bind using your favorite method or refer to Bonus Technique: Binding (page 100).

4. Make a label and sew it on the back of the quilt.

SUMMER ROMANCE

Nothing quite sweeps you off your feet like a summer romance. This quilt captures the essence of that romance with delicate flower petals dancing through the Dresdens as if blown by a warm summer breeze.

MATERIALS

White: 6½ yards for background and borders

Light blue border: 1 yard

Dark blue border: ⅝ yard

Blue leaves: 1¼ yards

Medium blue Dresdens: 1 yard total from at least 3 fabrics, using more fabrics for a scrappy look

Dark blue Dresdens: 2 yards total from at least 6 fabrics, using more fabrics for a scrappy look

Backing: 8½ yards

Binding: ⅞ yard

Batting: 98″ × 98″

CUTTING

Appliqué

Make templates A, B, and C using the *Summer Romance* patterns (page 80). Refer to Making Templates (page 7) as needed.

- Cut 13 center squares C from white.
- Cut 48 petals A from medium blue.
- Cut 108 petals A from dark blue.
- Cut 98 leaves B from blue leaves.

Background

- Cut 9 white strips 8¼″ × width of fabric; subcut 52 pieces 6⅞″ × 8¼″.
- Cut 2 white squares 21¼″ × 21¼″; cut diagonally twice to make 8 triangles for sides.
- Cut 2 white squares 10⅞″ × 10⅞″; cut diagonally once to make 4 triangles for corners.

CUTTING continued on page 76

Skill level:
intermediate

Finished quilt:
90½" × 90½"

Finished block:
6³/₈" × 7³/₄"

Summer Romance

CUTTING *continued*

Border 1

- Cut 7 white strips
  3″ × width of fabric, sew
  end to end, and subcut
  2 strips 3″ × 60½″ and
  2 strips 3″ × 65½″.

Border 2

- Cut 4 light blue corners
  8″ × 8″.

- Cut 88 white squares
  3″ × 3″.

- Cut 48 dark blue squares
  3″ × 3″.

- Cut 64 light blue squares
  3⅜″ × 3⅜″.

- Cut 44 white squares
  3⅜″ × 3⅜″.

- Cut 20 dark blue squares
  3⅜″ × 3⅜″.

Border 3

- Cut 9 white strips
  5½″ × length of fabric, sew
  end to end, and subcut
  2 strips 5½″ × 80½″ and
  2 strips 5½″ × 90½″.

Construction

Press after adding each border.

SEW TOGETHER THE PETALS

1. Sew together the 156 assorted medium and dark blue petals in random groups of 3 (refer to Sewing Dresden Petals Together, page 8).

2. After the petals are sewn together, press them using the *Summer Romance* Dresden pressing guide (page 81). Refer to Pressing and Blocking (page 12).

ASSEMBLE THE BLOCKS

1. Appliqué the petal set to the background rectangles (refer to Needle Turn Appliqué, page 8). Appliqué the bottom curve of each Dresden as well so the white shows through as with reverse appliqué (page 12).

2. Sew the first set to the center square C, leaving the seam unstitched ¾″ where indicated.

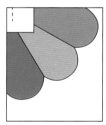

3. Add the second, third, and fourth sides.

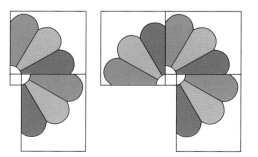

Designed by Marian Gallian and Yvette Marie Jones,
made by Marian Gallian and Nancy Butler, quilted by Kathryn Carbine

4. When sewing the last seam, include the ¾˝ left unstitched in Step 2.

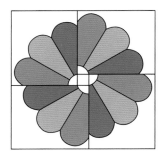

5. Join the squares and background triangles together in a diagonal grid.

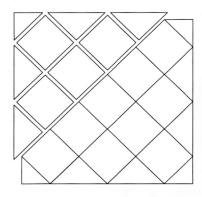

MAKE THE BORDERS

Border 1

1. Sew 2 white 3˝ × 60½˝ strips to opposite sides of the quilt.

2. Sew 2 white 3˝ × 65½˝ strips to the remaining sides of the quilt.

3. Appliqué the 98 leaves to the background.

Border 2

Refer to Half-Square Triangles (page 40) as needed.

1. Pair 44 white 3⅜˝ × 3⅜˝ squares with 44 light blue 3⅜˝ × 3⅜˝ squares, right sides together.

2. Draw a diagonal line from corner to corner on the back of the white squares.

3. Sew ¼˝ away on either side of the line.

4. Cut apart on the line and press the seam toward the light blue, making 88 half-square triangles.

5. Repeat Steps 1–4 with 20 light blue 3⅜˝ × 3⅜˝ squares and 20 dark blue 3⅜˝ × 3⅜˝ squares to make 40 half-square triangles. Press the seams toward the dark blue.

6. Sew 24 units A using 48 white 3″ × 3″ squares, 48 dark blue 3″ × 3″ squares, and 48 white/light blue half-square triangles.

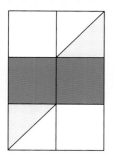

Make 24.

7. Sew 20 units B using 40 white 3″ × 3″ squares, 40 white/light blue half-square triangles, and 40 light blue/dark blue half-square triangles.

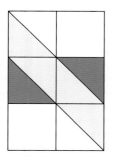

Make 20.

8. Referring to the diagram, arrange 4 borders, each with 6 units A and 5 units B, alternating.

9. Sew each border together.

10. Sew 2 borders from Step 9 to opposite sides of the quilt.

11. Sew 2 light blue 8″ × 8″ corners to each end of the remaining borders from Step 9.

12. Sew the borders from Step 11 to the remaining sides of the quilt.

Border 3

1. Sew 2 white 5½″ × 80½″ strips to opposite sides of the quilt.

2. Sew 2 white 5½″ × 90½″ strips to the remaining sides of the quilt.

FINISH THE QUILT

1. Layer the quilt top, batting, and backing.

2. Quilt as desired.

3. Bind using your favorite method or refer to Bonus Technique: Binding (page 100).

4. Make a label and sew it on the back of the quilt.

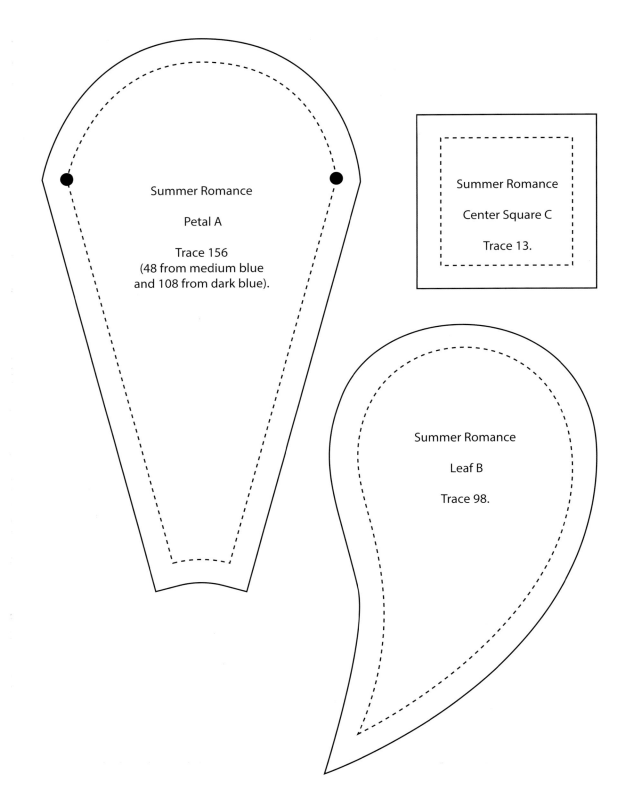

Summer Romance

Petal A

Trace 156
(48 from medium blue
and 108 from dark blue).

Summer Romance

Center Square C

Trace 13.

Summer Romance

Leaf B

Trace 98.

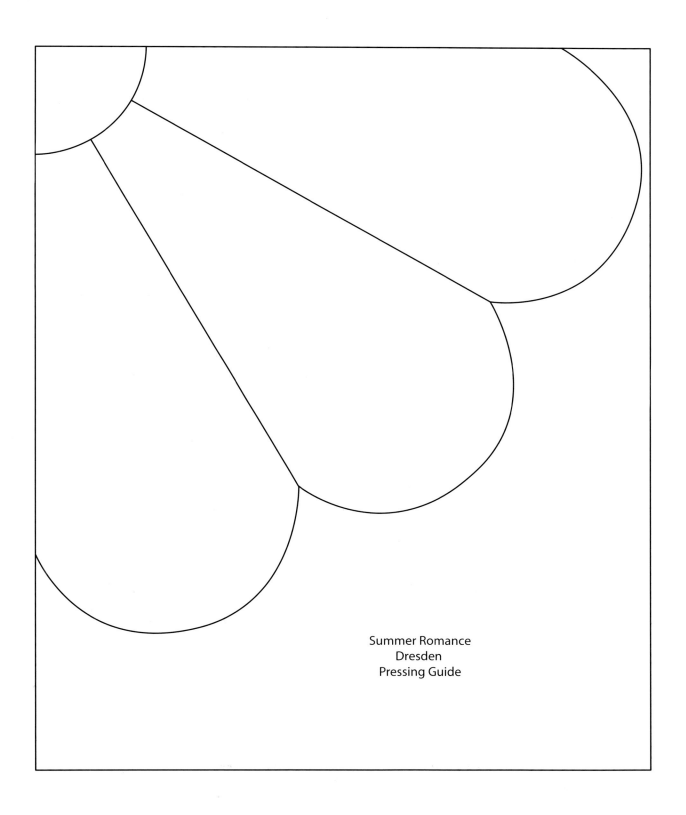

Summer Romance
Dresden
Pressing Guide

TERRACED GARDEN

Summer is a gardener's paradise, with annuals to plant and perennials in bloom. We designed this quilt from a bird's-eye view to capture a terraced flower bed filled with bright blue petals.

MATERIALS

Medium blue: 1¾ yards for petals

Multicolor blue: 2¾ yards for petals and borders 7 and 16

Medium dark blue: 1¾ yards for petals and border 18

Black: ⅝ yard for centers and border 19

White: ⅝ yard for center squares and border 1

Blue dots: 2¼ yards for borders 2, 6, 10, and 14

Gray with large black dots: ¾ yard for border 3

White with gray pop: 1¾ yards for borders 4 and 5

White with light gray: 2½ yards for borders 8 and 9

Gray with small black dots: 1⅛ yards for borders 11, 16, and 17

Gray with gray stars: 1⅜ yards for borders 12 and 13

Gray damask: ⅓ yard for border 15

White with black dots: 1½ yards for border 20

Black binding: 1 yard

Backing: 8¾ yards

Batting: 104″ × 104″

Skill level:
intermediate

Finished quilt:
96½" × 96½"

Finished block:
8" × 8"

CUTTING

Appliqué

Make templates A, B, C, and D using the *Terraced Garden* patterns (pullout pages P1, P2, and P4). Refer to Making Templates (page 7) as needed.

Petals

- Cut 8 strips 7″ × width of fabric from the medium blue; cut 72 petals A.
- Cut 8 strips 7″ × width of fabric from the multicolor blue; cut 72 petals A.
- Cut 8 strips 7″ × width of fabric from the medium dark blue; cut 72 petals A.

Black centers

- Cut 14 quarter-circles B.
- Cut 27 semicircles C.
- Cut 1 center circle D.

Center squares

- Cut 4 white squares 8½″ × 8½″.

Border 1

- Cut 2 white strips 3¾″ × width of fabric; subcut 2 strips 3¾″ × 16½″ and 2 strips 3¾″ × 23″.

Border 2

Note: Fussy cutting the dotted border strips means to note the position of the dots across the width of the strip and to cut all of them the same.

- Fussy cut 2 blue dot strips 2¼″ × 23″ from length of fabric.
- Fussy cut 2 blue dot strips 2¼″ × 26½″ from length of fabric.

Border 3

- Fussy cut 2 gray with large black dots strips 3½″ × 26½″ from width of fabric.
- Fussy cut 2 gray with large black dots strips 3½″ × 32½″ from width of fabric.

Border 4

- Cut 20 squares 8½″ × 8½″ from the white with gray pop.

Border 5

- Cut 5 strips 3¾″ × width of fabric using the white with gray pop, sew end to end, and cut 2 rectangles 3¾″ × 48½″ and 2 strips 3¾″ × 55″.

Border 6

From the blue dots:

- **Bottom:** Fussy cut 1 strip 2¼″ × 55″ from length of fabric.
- **Top:** Fussy cut 1 strip 2¼″ × 51½″ from length of fabric.
- **Left:** Fussy cut 1 strip 2¼″ × 58½″ from length of fabric.
- **Right:** Fussy cut 1 strip 2¼″ × 53½″ from length of fabric.

Border 7

- Cut 6 multicolor blue strips 3½″ × width of fabric, sew end to end, and subcut:

Bottom: 1 strip 3½″ × 58½″

Top: 1 strip 3½″ × 48½″

Left: 1 strip 3½″ × 60″

Right: 1 strip 3½″ × 52½″

Border 8

- Cut 28 squares 8½″ × 8½″ from the white with light gray print.

CUTTING continued on page 86

Designed by Marian Gallian, made by Marian Gallian and Nancy Butler, quilted by Kathryn Carbine
Fabric: Andrea Victoria 2 collection by Riley Blake Designs

CUTTING continued

Border 9

- Cut 5 strips 3¾″ × width of fabric from the white with light gray, sew end to end, and subcut:

  Bottom: 1 strip 3¾″ × 74½″

  Top: 1 strip 3¾″ × 26½″

  Left: 1 strip 3¾″ × 56½″

  Right: 1 strip 3¾″ × 40½″

Border 10

From the blue dots:

- **Bottom:** Fussy cut 1 strip 2¼″ × 74½″ from length of fabric.

- **Top:** Fussy cut 1 strip 2¼″ × 26½″ from length of fabric.

- **Left:** Fussy cut 1 strip 2¼″ × 56½″ from length of fabric.

- **Right:** Fussy cut 1 strip 2¼″ × 40½″ from length of fabric.

Border 11

- Fussy cut 5 strips 3½″ × width of fabric from the gray with small black dots, sew end to end, and fussy cut:

  Bottom: 1 strip 3½″ × 74½″

  Top: 1 strip 3½″ × 26½″

  Left: 1 strip 3½″ × 56½″

  Right: 1 strip 3½″ × 40½″

Border 12

- Cut 16 squares 8½″ × 8½″ from the gray with gray stars print.

Border 13

From the gray with gray stars print:

- **Bottom:** Cut 1 strip 3¾″ × 40½″.

- **Left:** Cut 1 strip 3¾″ × 24½″.

- **Right:** Cut 1 strip 3¾″ × 10″; center when stitching on.

Border 14

From the blue dots:

- **Bottom:** Fussy cut 1 strip 2¼″ × 40½″ from length of fabric.

- **Left:** Fussy cut 1 strip 2¼″ × 24½″ from length of fabric.

- **Right:** Fussy cut 1 strip 2¼″ × 10″ from length of fabric; center when stitching on.

Border 15

- **Bottom:** Cut 1 gray damask strip 3½″ × 40½″.

- **Left:** Cut 1 gray damask strip 3½″ × 24½″.

Border 16

- Fussy cut 4 squares 8½″ × 8½″ from the gray with small black dots.

Border 17

- Fussy cut 1 strip 3¾″ × 8½″ from the gray with small black dots.

Border 18

- Cut 1 medium dark blue strip 2″ × 8½″.

Border 19

- Cut 9 black strips 1″ × width of fabric, sew end to end, and subcut:

  2 strips 1″ × 88½″

  2 strips 1″ × 89½″

Border 20

- Fussy cut 10 strips 4″ × width of fabric from the white with large black dots, sew end to end, and fussy cut:

  2 strips 4″ × 89½″

  2 strips 4″ × 96½″

Construction

Press after sewing on each row of borders.

SEW TOGETHER THE PETALS

1. Sew the petals together into 72 identical sets of 3 (refer to Sewing Dresden Petals Together, page 8).

2. After the petals are sewn together, press them using the *Terraced Garden* Dresden pressing guide (pullout page P2). Refer to Pressing and Blocking (page 12).

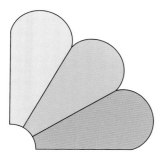

ASSEMBLE THE CENTER

1. Appliqué the petal sets onto the 4 white 8½″ × 8½″ squares (refer to Needle Turn Appliqué, page 8).

2. Sew the 4 blocks together, forming the center square.

3. Appliqué the center circle D.

MAKE THE BORDERS

Border 1

1. Sew the 2 white 3¾″ × 16½″ strips to opposite sides of the quilt.

2. Sew the 2 white 3¾″ × 23″ strips to the remaining sides of the quilt.

Border 2

1. Sew the 2 blue dot 2¼″ × 23″ strips to opposite sides of the quilt.

2. Sew the 2 blue dot 2¼″ × 26½″ strips to the remaining sides of the quilt.

Border 3

1. Sew the 2 strips 3½″ × 26½″ from the gray with large black dots to opposite sides of the quilt.

2. Sew the 2 strips 3½″ × 32½″ from the gray with large black dots to the remaining sides of the quilt.

Border 4

1. Appliqué 20 petal sets onto the 20 squares 8½″ × 8½″ from the white with gray pop.

2. Sew 8 pairs together and appliqué a half-circle C on them.

3. On the remaining 4, appliqué a quarter-circle B.

4. Sew 2 rows of 4 as shown and sew to opposite sides.

Note

Notice how the Dresdens line up through the center.

5. Sew 2 rows of 6 as shown and sew to the remaining sides.

Border 5

Beginning with this border, you will see the quilt beginning to take shape. You can now mark the top of the quilt. All rows will now be marked top, bottom, left, and right, indicating the side they will be sewn on. As you sew on the rows, do not trim until you reach row 18.

1. Sew the 2 gray pop 3¾″ × 48½″ strips to the top and bottom of the quilt.

2. Sew the 2 gray pop 3¾″ × 55″ strips to the left and right sides of the quilt.

Border 6

1. **Bottom:** Sew 1 blue dot 2¼″ × 55″ strip to the bottom.

2. **Top:** Sew 1 blue dot 2¼″ × 51½″ strip to the top side, aligning one end to the left side.

3. **Left:** Sew 1 blue dot 2¼″ × 58½″ strip to the left side.

4. **Right:** Sew 1 blue dot 2¼″ × 53½″ strip to the right side, aligning one end to the bottom.

Border 7

1. **Bottom:** Sew 1 multicolor 3½″ × 58½″ strip to the bottom.

2. **Top:** Center and sew 1 multicolor 3½″ × 48½″ strip to the top side.

3. **Left:** Sew 1 multicolor 3½″ × 60″ strip to the left side, aligning one end to the bottom.

4. **Right:** Sew 1 multicolor 3½″ × 52½″ strip to the right side, aligning one end to the bottom.

Border 8

1. Appliqué 28 petal sets onto the 28 light gray 8½″ × 8½″ squares.

2. Sew 12 pairs together and appliqué a half-circle C on each.

3. Appliqué a quarter-circle B on the remaining 4.

4. Referring to diagram, sew together 5 for the top, 6 for the right, 7 for the left, and 10 for the bottom.

5. Sew the borders to each side, keeping the petal sets in line with the previous petal borders.

Border 9

1. **Bottom:** Sew 1 white with light gray 3¾″ × 74½″ strip to the bottom, aligning one end to the left side.

2. **Top:** Center and sew 1 white with light gray 3¾″ × 26½″ strip to the top side.

3. **Left:** Sew 1 white with light gray 3¾″ × 56½″ strip to the left side, aligning one end to the bottom.

4. **Right:** Center and sew 1 white with light gray 3¾″ × 40½″ strip to the right side.

Border 10

1. **Bottom:** Center and sew 1 blue dot 2¼″ × 74½″ strip to the bottom.

2. **Top:** Center and sew 1 blue dot 2¼″ × 26½″ strip to the top.

3. **Left:** Center and sew 1 blue dot 2¼″ × 56½″ strip to the left side.

4. **Right:** Center and sew 1 blue dot 2¼″ × 40½″ strip to the right side.

Border 11

1. **Bottom:** Center and sew 1 strip 3½″ × 74½″ from the gray with small black dots to the bottom.

2. **Top:** Center and sew 1 strip 3½″ × 26½″ from the gray with small black dots to the top side.

3. **Left:** Center and sew 1 strip 3½″ × 56½″ from the gray with small black dots to the left side.

4. **Right:** Center and sew 1 strip 3½″ × 40½″ from the gray with small black dots to the right side.

Border 12

1. Appliqué 16 petal sets onto the 16 squares 8½″ × 8½″ from the gray with gray stars print.

2. Sew 6 pairs together and appliqué a half-circle C on each.

3. Appliqué a quarter-circle B on the remaining 4.

4. Referring to the diagram, sew together 3 for the right, 5 for the left, and 7 for the bottom.

5. Sew 1 on the top and the remaining borders to each side, keeping the petal sets in line with the previous petal borders.

Border 13

1. **Bottom:** Center and sew 1 strip 3¾″ × 40½″ from the gray with gray stars print to the bottom.

2. **Left:** Center and sew 1 strip 3¾″ × 24½″ from the gray with gray stars to the left.

3. **Right:** Center and sew 1 strip 3¾″ × 10″ from the gray with gray stars to the right.

Border 14

1. **Bottom:** Center and sew 1 blue dot strip 2¼″ × 40½″ to the bottom.

2. **Left:** Center and sew 1 blue dot strip 2¼″ × 24½″ to the left.

3. **Right:** Center and sew 1 blue dot strip 2¼″ × 10″ to the right.

Border 15

1. **Bottom:** Center and sew 1 gray damask 3½″ × 40½″ strip to the bottom.

2. **Left:** Center and sew 1 gray damask 3½″ × 24½″ strip to the left side.

Border 16

1. Appliqué 4 petal sets onto the 4 squares 8½″ × 8½″ from the gray with small black dots.

2. Sew 1 pair together and appliqué a half-circle C.

3. Appliqué a quarter-circle B on the remaining blocks.

4. Sew 3 blocks together and sew to the bottom.

5. Sew 1 block to the left.

Border 17

Center and sew 1 strip 3¾″ × 8½″ from the gray with small black dots to the bottom.

Border 18

Sew a 2″ × 8½″ strip of medium blue fabric to the bottom.

Border 19

1. Begin trimming the quilt, starting with the top right side. Trim at a 45° angle just inside the ends of the border seam. Measure 88½″ centered on this side. Measure 88½″ from each corner across to the bottom and left corners. Mark the 4 corners. Adjust the marks until each side measures 88½″ and the corners are square. Sew the first black 1″ × 88½″ strip to the trimmed top right side right away. These are bias edges that will stretch and distort your quilt, so be gentle with them.

2. Trim the bottom left corner next and sew on the black 1″ × 88½″ strip.

3. Trim the remaining 2 sides and sew on the black 1″ × 89½″ strips.

BORDER 20

1. Sew 2 strips 4″ × 89½″ from the white with large black dots to opposite sides of the quilt.

2. Sew 2 strips 4″ × 96½″ from the white with large black dots to the remaining sides of the quilt.

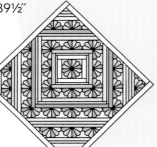

FINISH THE QUILT

1. Layer the quilt top, batting, and backing.

2. Quilt as desired.

3. Bind using your favorite method or refer to Bonus Technique: Binding (page 100).

4. Make a label and sew it on the back of the quilt.

BONUS PROJECT:
WINDOW BOX

Designed and made by Marian Gallian and Nancy Butler, quilted by Kathryn Carbine • *Fabrics: Andrea Victoria 2 collection by Riley Blake Designs*

Finished block: 8″ × 8″

Finished quilt: 48″ × 48″

Skill level: confident beginner

This quilt is a smaller version of the Terraced Garden. The center and first three borders are similar to Terraced Garden, but different widths. The fifth border has only twelve Dresdens, alternating with plain squares, and they face the opposite direction.

MATERIALS

Medium light petal: ½ yard

Medium dark blue petal: ½ yard

Multicolor petal: ½ yard

White: ⅝ yard

Blue dots: ⅞ yard

Gray with large black dots on gray: ⅜ yard

Black: ¼ yard

Gray pop: 1½ yards

Stripe binding: ½ yard

Backing: 3¼ yards

Batting: 56″ × 56″

CUTTING

Appliqué

Make templates A, B, C, and D using the *Terraced Garden* patterns (pullout pages P1, P2, and P4). Refer to Making Templates (page 7) as needed.

Petals

- **Medium light petal:** Cut 2 strips 7″ × width of fabric; cut 16 petals A.
- **Medium dark petal:** Cut 2 strips 7″ × width of fabric; cut 16 petals A.
- **Multicolor petal:** Cut 2 strips 7″ × width of fabric; cut 16 petals A.

Black centers

- Cut 4 quarter-circles B.
- Cut 4 semicircles C.
- Cut 1 center circle D.

Center squares

- Cut 4 white squares 8½″ × 8½″.

Border 1

- Cut 2 white strips 3¼″ × width of fabric; subcut 2 strips 3¼″ × 16½″ and 2 strips 3¼″ × 22″.

Border 2

- Fussy cut 2 blue dot strips 2½″ × 22″ from length of fabric.
- Fussy cut 2 blue dot strips 2½″ × 26″ from length of fabric.

Border 3

- Fussy cut 2 strips 2½″ × 26″ from width of fabric using the gray with large black dots.
- Fussy cut 2 strips 2½″ × 30″ from width of fabric using the gray with large black dots.

Border 4

- Cut 2 black strips 1½″ × 30″ from width of fabric.
- Cut 2 black strips 1½″ × 32″ from width of fabric.

Border 5

- Cut 20 gray pop squares 8½″ × 8½″.

Construction

See Sew Together the Petals, Assemble the Center, and Make the Borders (page 87) in *Terraced Garden*, adding the black border before *Terraced Garden*'s border 4.

WINDSWEPT

As summer draws to a close and the petals and leaves start to fall to the ground, a cool fall breeze sweeps the last remnants of the season away. This quilt celebrates the end of summer and the beginning of fall, with its floating leaves and swirling flowers bridging the gap from one season to the next.

MATERIALS

Gold 1: 1 yard for petals

Cream/gray/gold print 1: 1 yard for petals

Cream/gray/gold print 2: ¼ yard for centers

Cream: 3 yards for background and border 2

Gray 1: ½ yard for leaves

Gold 2: ½ yard for leaves

Gray 2: ⅓ yard for border 1

Gray stripe: 2½ yards for border 3

Binding: ¾ yard

Backing: 7⅓ yards

Batting: 88″ × 88″

CUTTING

Appliqué

Make templates A through J using the *Windswept* patterns (pages 97–99). Refer to Making Templates (page 7) as needed.

Large petals

- Cut 6 large blades A from gold 1.
- Cut 6 large blades A from cream/gray/gold print 1.
- Cut 6 large blades B from gold 1.
- Cut 6 large blades B from cream/gray/gold print 1.

Medium petals

- Cut 12 medium blades D from gold 1.
- Cut 12 medium blades D from cream/gray/gold print 1.
- Cut 12 medium blades E from gold 1.
- Cut 12 medium blades E from cream/gray/gold print 1.

CUTTING continued on page 94

CUTTING continued

Small petals

- Cut 12 small blades G from gold 1.
- Cut 12 small blades G from cream/gray/gold print 1.
- Cut 12 small blades H from gold 1.
- Cut 12 small blades H from cream/gray/gold print 1.

Center circles

- Cut 1 large circle C from cream/gray/gold print 2.
- Cut 2 medium circles F from cream/gray/gold print 2.
- Cut 2 small circles I from cream/gray/gold print 2.

Leaves

- Cut 13 leaves J from gray 1.
- Cut 13 leaves J from gold 2.

Center background: Cut 5 cream strips 13″ × width of fabric, sew end to end, and cut 4 rectangles 13″ × 50½″.

Border 1: Cut 6 gray strips 1½″ × width of fabric, sew end to end, and cut 2 rectangles 1½″ × 50½″ and 2 rectangles 1½″ × 52½″.

Border 2: Cut 6 cream strips 6½″ × width of fabric, sew end to end, and cut 2 rectangles 6½″ × 52½″ and 2 rectangles 6½″ × 64½″.

Border 3: Cut 9 gray stripe strips 8½″ × width of fabric, sew end to end, and cut 4 rectangles 8½″ × 86″.

Construction

Press after adding each border.

PREPARE THE PETALS

Place the appliqués on the individual blades and appliqué the curve (refer to Needle Turn Appliqué, page 8).

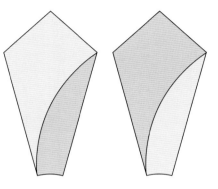

DRESDEN FLOWERS

1. Sew together 12 Dresden petals of similar size, alternating colors to create the wave and forming each of the 5 Dresden flowers.

2. Appliqué the 1 large Dresden center C to the large flower.

3. Appliqué the 2 medium Dresden centers F to the medium flowers.

4. Appliqué the 2 small Dresden centers I to the small flowers.

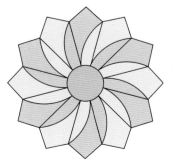

Designed by Yvette Marie Jones and Marian Gallian, made by Marian Gallian and Nancy Butler, quilted by Kathryn Carbine • *Fabric: Lost and Found 2 collection by Riley Blake Designs*

ALTERNATE COLORWAY: *Summer Breeze Quilt*

Designed by Yvette Marie Jones and Marian Gallian, made by Marian Gallian and Nancy Butler, quilted by Kathryn Carbine

SEW FLOWERS AND PETALS TO BACKGROUND

1. Place the 4 cream center rectangles on a design wall, overlapping by ½˝.

2. Pin all appliqués to the cream pieces. (Don't worry if some straddle the edges of the background pieces.)

3. Appliqué each section. For any pieces that straddle 2 sections, leave the biggest part of those pieces pinned to one section and leave the other half of the appliqué until later when the sections are sewn together. Don't appliqué closer than 1˝ from the unsewn seams.

4. Sew the 4 sections together.

5. Appliqué all the pieces that are straddling 2 sections.

Note

This quilt was designed to have a windswept feel, so exact placement is not necessary to achieve the effect.

MAKE THE BORDERS

Border 1

1. Sew 2 gray 1½″ × 50½″ strips to opposite sides of the quilt.

2. Sew 2 gray 1½″ × 52½″ strips to the remaining sides of the quilt.

Border 2

1. Sew 2 cream 6½″ × 52½″ pieces to opposite sides of the quilt.

2. Sew 2 cream 6½″ × 64½″ pieces to the remaining sides of the quilt.

3. Finish appliquéing the pieces to the quilt top.

Border 3

1. Center and sew the 4 gray stripe 8½″ × 86″ pieces to all 4 sides of the quilt, stopping ¼″ from the each end on every side.

2. Miter the corners.

Mitering Border Corners

1. Center and pin border strips in place. Begin and end seams ¼″ from the edge of the fabric and backstitch.

2. Place the quilt on an ironing board and fold each border back along the 45° diagonal and press.

3. Fold the quilt diagonally with right sides together, aligning the pressed creases of the borders. Stitch along the crease.

4. Press the seams and check the quilt for accuracy. Trim excess fabric to ¼″.

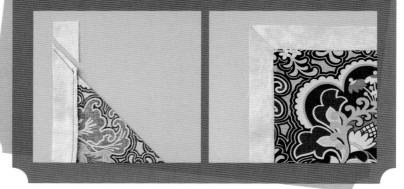

FINISH THE QUILT

1. Layer the quilt top, batting, and backing.

2. Quilt as desired.

3. Bind using your favorite method or refer to Bonus Technique: Binding (page 100).

4. Make a label and sew it on the back of the quilt.

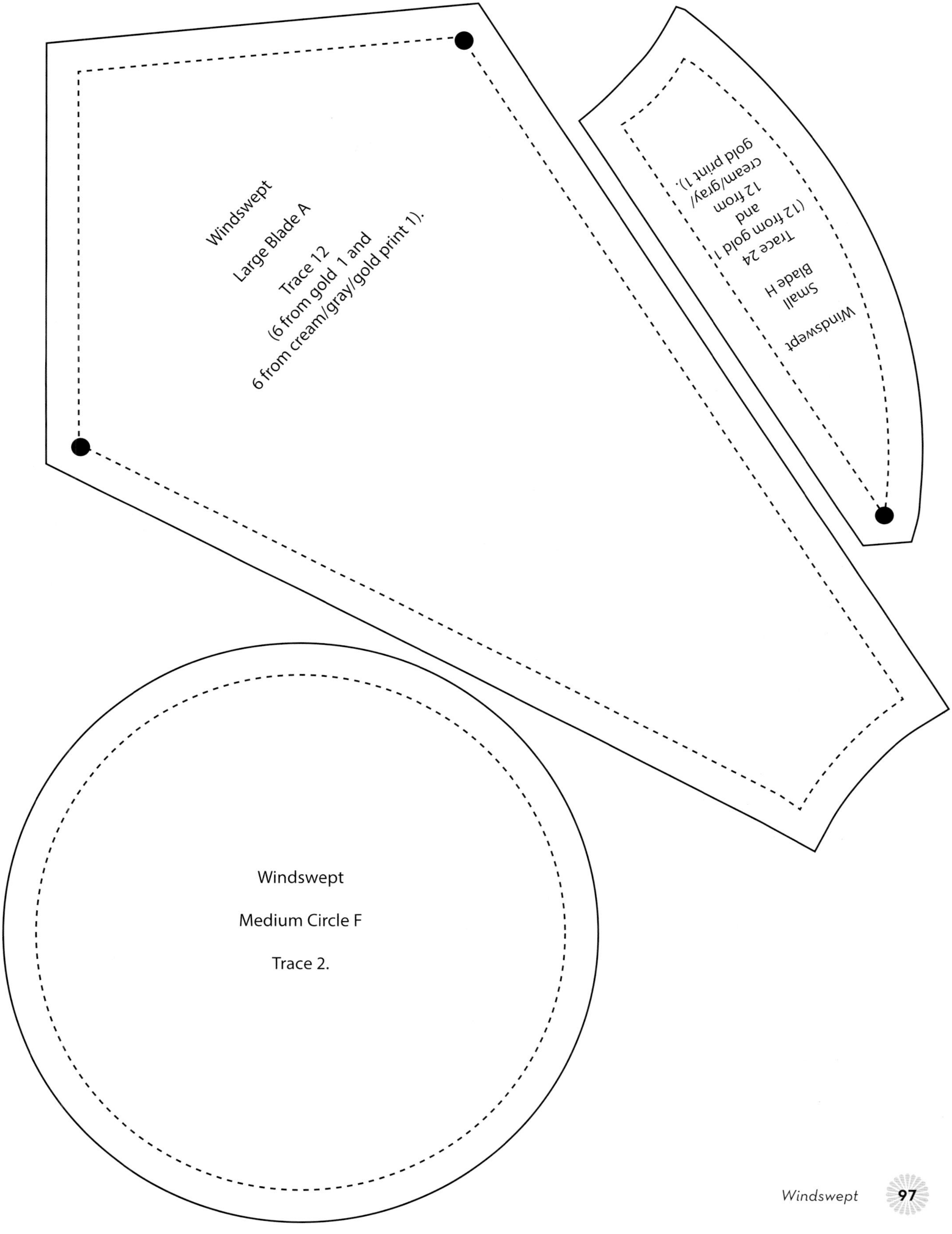

Windswept

Large Blade A

Trace 12
(6 from gold 1 and
6 from cream/gray/gold print 1).

Windswept
Small
Blade H
Trace 24
(12 from gold 1
and
12 from
cream/gray/
gold print 1).

Windswept

Medium Circle F

Trace 2.

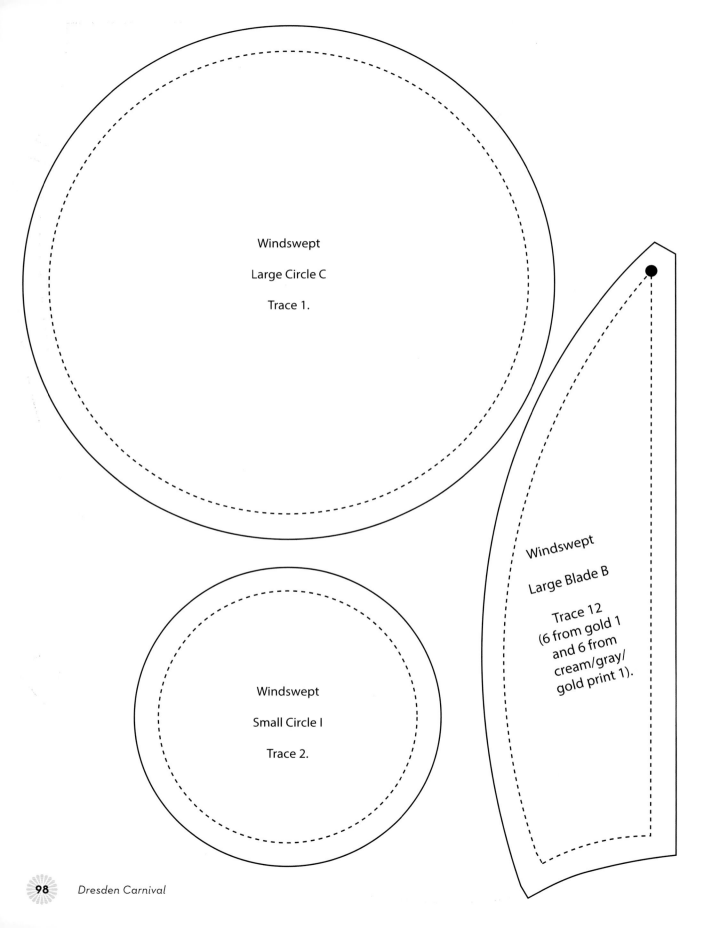

Windswept

Large Circle C

Trace 1.

Windswept

Large Blade B

Trace 12
(6 from gold 1
and 6 from
cream/gray/
gold print 1).

Windswept

Small Circle I

Trace 2.

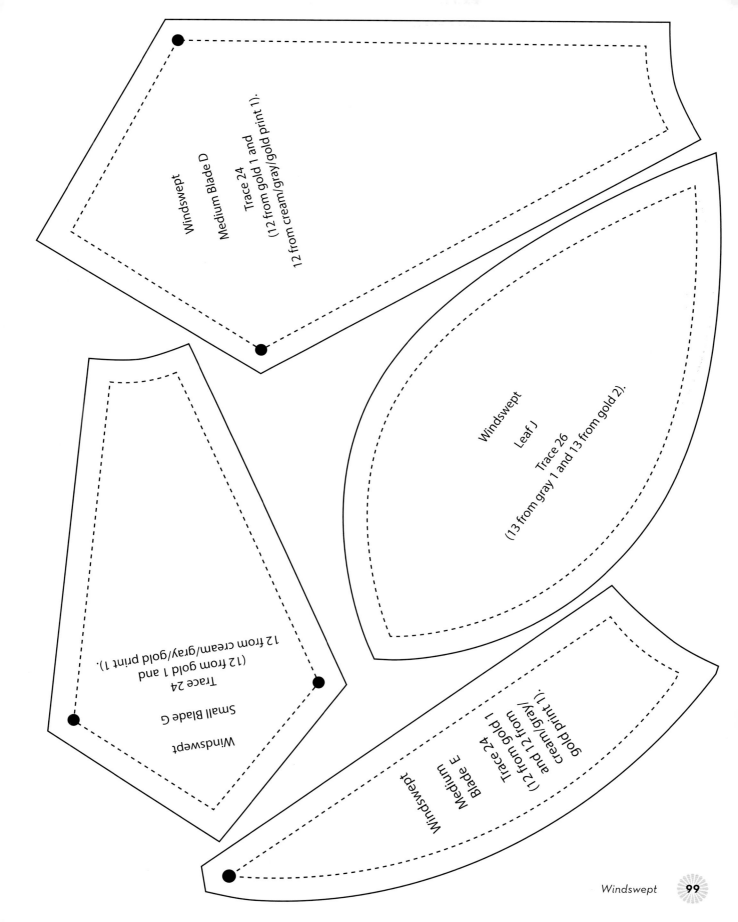

Windswept

Medium Blade D

Trace 24
(12 from gold 1 and
12 from cream/gray/gold print 1).

Windswept

Leaf J

Trace 26
(13 from gray 1 and 13 from gold 2).

Windswept

Small Blade G

Trace 24
(12 from gold 1 and
12 from cream/gray/gold print 1).

Windswept

Medium
Blade E

Trace 24
(12 from gold 1
and 12 from
cream/gray/
gold print 1).

BONUS TECHNIQUE: BINDING

Trim excess batting and backing from the quilt even with the edges of the quilt top.

Double-Fold Straight-Grain Binding

If you want a ¼˝ finished binding, cut the binding strips 1⅝˝ wide and piece them together with diagonal seams to make a continuous binding strip. Trim the seam allowances to ¼˝. Press the seams open.

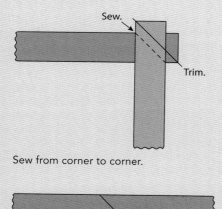

Sew from corner to corner.

Completed diagonal seam

Press the entire strip in half lengthwise with wrong sides together. With raw edges even, pin the binding to the front edge of the quilt a few inches away from a corner, and leave the first few inches of the binding unattached. Start sewing, using a ¼˝ seam allowance.

Stop ¼˝ away from the first corner (see Step 1), and backstitch 1 stitch. Lift the presser foot and needle. Rotate the quilt one-quarter turn. Fold the binding at a right angle so it extends straight above the quilt and the fold forms a 45° angle in the corner (see Step 2). Then bring the binding strip down even with the edge of the quilt (see Step 3). Begin sewing at the folded edge. Repeat in the same manner at all corners.

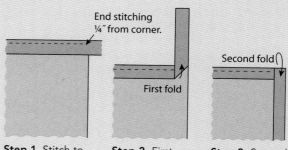

Step 1. Stitch to ¼˝ from corner.

Step 2. First fold for miter

Step 3. Second fold alignment

Continue stitching until you are back near the beginning of the binding strip. See Finishing the Binding Ends (page 102) for tips on finishing and hiding the raw edges of the ends of the binding.

Continuous Bias Binding

A continuous bias binding involves using a square sliced in half diagonally and then sewing the triangles together so that you continuously cut marked strips to make continuous bias binding. The same instructions can be used to cut bias for piping.

To determine the size of the square:

1. Multiply the strip width by the total length of the binding needed plus 16″ for seams. Find the square root of this number.

2. Multiply the strip width by 1.414 for longer segments.

3. Add the numbers from Steps 1 and 2. The total is the size of the square.

Example: For 2½″ binding for a 110″ quilt, you will need a 20″ × 20″ square.

2.5″ × 110″ = 275 sq. in.

$\sqrt{275}$ sq. in. = 16.58″

2.5″ × 1.414 = 3.5″

16.58″ + 3.5″ = 20″

Cut the square and cut in half diagonally. Sew these triangles together as shown, using a ¼″ seam allowance. Press the seam open.

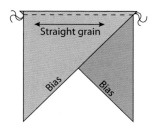

Sew triangles together.

Using a ruler, mark the parallelogram created by the 2 triangles with lines spaced the width you need to cut your bias. Cut about 5″ along the first line.

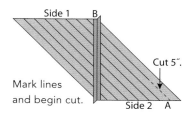

Join Side 1 and Side 2 to form a tube. The raw edge at point A will align with the raw edge at B. This will allow the first line to be offset by 1 strip width. Pin the raw edges right sides together, making sure that the drawn lines match. Sew with a ¼″ seam allowance. Press the seam open. Cut along the drawn lines, creating 1 continuous strip.

Press the entire strip in half lengthwise with wrong sides together. Place the binding on the quilt as described in Double-Fold Straight-Grain Binding (above).

See Finishing the Binding Ends for tips on finishing and hiding the raw edges of the ends of the binding.

Finishing the Binding Ends

METHOD 1

After stitching around the quilt, fold under the beginning tail of the binding strip ¼″ so that the raw edge will be inside the binding after it is turned to the back of the quilt. Place the end tail of the binding strip over the beginning folded end. Continue to attach the binding and stitch slightly beyond the starting stitches. Trim the excess binding. Fold the binding over the raw edges to the quilt back and hand stitch, mitering the corners.

METHOD 2

Refer to ctpub.com > Quiltmaking Basics and Sewing Tips > Completing a Binding with an Invisible Seam.

Fold the ending tail of the binding back on itself where it meets the beginning binding tail. From the fold, measure and mark the cut width of your binding strip. Cut the ending binding tail to this measurement. For example, if your binding is cut 2⅛″ wide, measure from the fold on the ending tail of the binding 2⅛″ and cut the binding tail to this length.

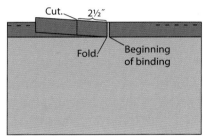

Cut binding tail.

Open both tails. Place one tail on top of the other at right angles, right sides together. Mark a diagonal line from corner to corner and stitch on the line. Check that you've done it correctly and that the binding fits the quilt; then trim the seam allowance to ¼″. Press open.

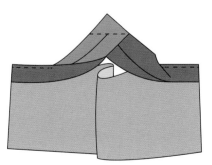

Refold the binding and stitch this binding section in place on the quilt. Fold the binding over the raw edges to the quilt back and hand stitch.

ABOUT THE AUTHORS

Marian Gallian

As Marian was growing up, she watched her mom cut and sew fabric at the kitchen table every day. Everything she and her mom wore was sewn by Mom. And thus a fascination with sewing and fabric began. A college degree in accounting took her in a different direction for a time, but now those skills with numbers only add to her pattern designing and writing skills. A minor in art gave her an appreciation and love for all forms of art.

She started her own company, Pink Hippo Quilts, specializing in original quilt patterns. This later became a springboard to a second business, Quilt St. George, an annual winter quilting retreat in St. George, Utah.

Marian grew up in the San Francisco Bay Area and now resides near Salt Lake City, Utah. She has seven children and more than twenty grandchildren.

Resources

JEANA KIMBALL'S FOXGLOVE COTTAGE
Appliqué supplies including straw needles
jeanakimballquilter.com/store

C&T PUBLISHING
Essential Self-Adhesive Laminating Sheets, Essential Appliqué Pins, and other quiltmaking supplies • ctpub.com

Yvette Marie Jones

Art and design have always been a large part of Yvette's life. She was taught and inspired at a young age by her mother, Marian Gallian, who shared her love of art and sewing with her and encouraged her to pursue her talents. At the age of thirteen, Yvette enrolled in her first graphic design class at the local college and has been hooked on design ever since.

A few years ago Yvette started teaming up with her mother to design quilts, which eventually led to her starting her own company called Vetmari (named after the nickname her mother always calls her that is short for Yvette Marie). Vetmari specializes in surface pattern design and graphic design as well as patterns for quiltmaking, sewing, and embroidery. Yvette has also licensed her designs for quilting fabric and home decor products. Her style is feminine and modern, and she loves to draw inspiration from vintage motifs.

Yvette grew up in picturesque St. George, Utah and now resides in Northern Utah with her husband and two children.

Visit us at **ctpub.com** and receive a special offer

For inspiring content that keeps you smiling and sewing

Find out what's new at C&T PUBLISHING

FREE Projects ▪ FREE How-to Videos
Blog ▪ Books ▪ Patterns ▪ Tools ▪ Rulers
Templates ▪ TAP Transfer Artist Paper
kraft•tex™ ▪ & more

Go to ctpub.com/offer

Sign up and receive your special offer